Gospel T

Anthony Freeman studied Che
College, Oxford, and trained for the pri
Ordained in 1972, he held a variety of pastoral and educational
posts until his dismissal by the Bishop of Chichester following
the publication of *God in Us* (SCM Press, 1993). Currently the
managing editor of the *Journal of Consciousness Studies*, he writes
and lectures on this subject as well as theology. He remains a
priest in the Church of England.

GOSPEL
TREASURE

Anthony Freeman

First published in Great Britain in 1999 by
Society for Promoting Christian Knowledge
Holy Trinity Church
Marylebone Road
London NW1 4DU

Scripture quotations, unless otherwise indicated,
are taken from the Oxford Anglicized edition of the
New Revised Standard Version of the Bible © 1989

British Library Cataloguing-in-Publication Data

A catalogue record for this book is available
from the British Library

ISBN 0–281–05267–0

Typeset by Wilmaset Ltd, Birkenhead, Wirral
Printed in Great Britain by
Redwood Books, Trowbridge, Wiltshire

For Jacqueline

Contents

Introduction: Four for the Gospel makers   1

1. Bethlehem   5
2. The baptism of Jesus   12
3. The temptations of Jesus   18
4. 'Your sins are forgiven'   26
5. The parable of the Sower   33
6. The Lord's Prayer (1)   40
7. The Lord's Prayer (2)   46
8. Feeding the five thousand (1)   55
9. Feeding the five thousand (2)   62
10. The Good Samaritan   71
11. Lazarus   79
12. The anointing of Jesus   86
13. Gospel truth   93

Introduction:
Four for the Gospel makers

The four Gospels – Matthew, Mark, Luke and John – stand at the centre of the Christian tradition. All Christians are bound to take them seriously. In the first instance that means taking them seriously at face value as eyewitness accounts of events in the life of Jesus. This book is a collection of Bible studies, for use by groups or individuals, which starts by doing exactly that. We shall listen to what the four Gospel writers have to tell us on basic questions like 'Where was Jesus born?' and 'What was the original wording of the Lord's Prayer?' No answers will be ruled out just because they seem to conflict with modern ideas or scientific attitudes. Only questions thrown up by a straightforward reading of the Gospels themselves will be explored.

Many Christians feel uncomfortable with the idea that the Gospels, which are proverbially true, might contain any factual errors or inconsistencies. Even to raise such questions is felt to indicate a lack of faith. However, that such questions do arise has been recognized from the earliest days of Christianity. Indeed, a special interest has always been taken in the apparent mistakes that occur in the Bible. This book is written in the firm belief that acknowledging and exploring these matters is a proper and essential part of Christian Bible study. My chief purpose is to encourage such study as a way of getting to know the Gospel writers better, and so to hear their message more clearly. No one should feel that in these pages the Bible is somehow being subjected to improper or sceptical scrutiny. That is why each chapter begins by treating the Gospels as historical records, and only when problems arise from within the pages of Scripture itself do we move on to seek solutions to these. When difficulties do arise from a purely historical approach to

1

the Gospels, we shall not ignore them, but ask what other motives the four evangelists might have had, beyond the mere recording of events.

Ancient and mediaeval scholars took biblical errors to be signposts, indicating that there was hidden treasure below for those who were prepared to dig for it. They assumed that any such error must be a deliberate hint from God that the true interpretation of this particular verse was not to be found in its obvious surface meaning, but should be understood as an ethical or mystical truth to be discovered only by prayerful study. We may find fanciful the idea that God would deliberately introduce mistakes into the Bible in order to teach us hidden spiritual truths. However, it does remain true that the Bible often comes alive precisely at those points where we hit problems, and exploring them opens up the real excitement and inspiration of the Scriptures.

It is in the spirit of these ancient Christian writers that I approach the Gospels. I assume they are historically accurate until confronted by internal contradictions. When that happens, I try to let the Scriptures tell their own story and in their own way. What clues are there in the text itself to tell us what is motivating the writer at this point? Is it possible that he was trying to be historically accurate and simply got it wrong? Or was his account perhaps being driven by some other concern? If so, what might that be? Only then does a further question arise: if the evangelist was indeed concerned with something other than eyewitness accuracy at point X in his story, where some internal discrepancy alerted us to it, what about the rest of his Gospel? It may be that elsewhere also, even without some obvious inconsistency, we need to look beyond the mere historical account if the Gospels are to yield us their treasures. Even then, it is the internal evidence of the Scriptures, not some modern idea of what might or might not be authentic, which will motivate our exploration.

To make my own assumptions clear, I do not doubt for a moment that the Gospels contain material that is historically accurate alongside other material that is historically dubious. What I do doubt is the possibility of ever accurately distinguishing the one from the other. That is why I do not engage in the so-called 'quest for the historical Jesus'. I invite the reader to undertake the different – and I believe more profitable – task of seeking the treasure below the historical surface of the Gospels as a whole. If I have a particular bias in my approach to the text, it is perhaps to be more influenced than most commentators by the significance of omissions and silences. For example, every writer about Mark's Gospel discusses the reasons why it has two accounts of Jesus feeding the multitude. I find it equally fascinating that it does not have any record at all of the parable of the Good Samaritan. In consequence, some of the passages discussed in these pages are ones where the differences between the accounts in two Gospels could easily be explained on the grounds that one or other evangelist simply omitted something. But for me that only raises the further question, Why did he omit this particular something? And why did the other writer include it?

For this book I have chosen to study topics from Jesus' life which are important but not necessarily controversial. This should make it easier for us to approach them with an open mind. In particular I have avoided two subjects: the virgin birth and the resurrection of Jesus. This is because – on any interpretation which takes them seriously – both of these are 'events' which cut through the normal course of history and human affairs. We shall find that we have quite enough to keep us busy without disturbing these deep waters.

All that is needed to engage in these studies is a Bible. Some readers may find it helpful to have a concordance – which is really just an index to the Bible – and a synopsis – a book in which the Gospels are printed in parallel columns – for checking the points made as we go along, but these are optional extras.*

* The word 'synopsis' means 'a general view', which is what the parallel printing of the Gospels gives the reader. The associated term 'synoptic' is used by scholars as a shorthand to refer jointly to the Gospels of Matthew, Mark and Luke. This reflects the fact that these three give an account of the events from the same general point of view, often seeming to agree together against John's account. To save undue repetition of 'Matthew, Mark and Luke', this shorthand will sometimes be used in this book.

The only essential requirement is a curiosity to know more about the Gospels, and a willingness to let them speak for themselves and so yield their treasure.

1

Bethlehem

Read: Matthew 1.18—2.23; Mark 1.9, 16–28; 2.1; 6.1–6;
Luke 1.26–32; 2.1–7, 21–24, 39; John 1.43–51; 2.12; 7.40–52

To begin at the beginning: where was Jesus born? Our Christmas carols give us the name of a place – the 'little town of Bethlehem' – and also hint at the significance of its being 'royal David's city'. However, the figure at the centre of these Bible studies is not known to history as 'Jesus of Bethelehem' but as 'Jesus of Nazareth'. Why is this? What is the evidence that he was really born in Bethlehem? It is a minor puzzle, but one that offers an interesting way into the world of the four evangelists. Taking each Gospel in turn, we shall find that Matthew and Luke offer solutions to this puzzle, while John leaves it unresolved and Mark appears to be unaware of it.

The events leading up to the birth of Jesus are told in Matthew 1.18–25, and there is no mention of where Mary and Joseph live. There is one possible clue, when the angel in Joseph's dream refers to him as 'Joseph, son of David' (echoing the information in the family tree with which the chapter begins). This could be taken as a hint that they lived in or near King David's family town of Bethlehem, and this possibility is confirmed in Matthew 2.1, where we read that 'Jesus was born in Bethlehem of Judea'.

There follows the familiar story of the visit of the wise men, of Herod's anger, and of the consequent flight of the holy family into the safety of Egypt. Then, in 2.19–23, Matthew answers our question about Jesus' association with Nazareth. He tells how Joseph returned to Israel after the death of Herod, but was still afraid to go back to Judea. Instead, he went north to Galilee and there 'he made his home in a town called Nazareth'.

Matthew's account is clear and simple: Jesus' family originally lived in Bethlehem, where he was born, and following a period abroad made a new home for themselves in Nazareth, after which he was named. The puzzle is solved.

Unlike Matthew, Mark gives no account of Jesus' birth or childhood. Jesus first arrives on the scene at the river Jordan in Mark 1.9, presumably already a grown man, 'from Nazareth of Galilee'. He begins his ministry in Galilee and is called 'Jesus of Nazareth' by the demoniac at Capernaum (Mark 1.24), which is the place he appears to make his base (Mark 2.1).

Mark never mentions Bethlehem, nor does he say explicitly that Jesus ever returned to Nazareth, but at 6.1 he writes that Jesus 'came to his [unnamed] home town'. It was not a happy occasion. The neighbours were scornful, despite his growing reputation as a teacher and healer, because they knew him and his family so well. It prompted Jesus to reflect that, 'Prophets are not without honour, except in their home town, and among their own kin, and in their own house' (Mark 6.4).

So Mark shows no apparent interest in Bethlehem, nor embarrassment at the fact that Jesus comes from Nazareth/ Galilee. For him there is no puzzle.

Luke in his first two chapters gives the account of Jesus' birth which is probably the most familiar. He tells us that from the outset Mary and Joseph lived at 'a town in Galilee called Nazareth'. It was there that the angel Gabriel announced to Mary that Jesus was to be her son; it was there that Jesus was brought up; and it was there that he would have been born, but for the imperial registration which required the family to visit Bethlehem just at the crucial time (Luke 2.1–4).

Their movements are not spelled out in detail, but forty days after the birth they were at the Temple in Jerusalem for their purification. It is possible they returned home in the interim, but perhaps more likely that they remained a few weeks in Bethlehem from where they made the short journey to Jerusalem for the ceremony. What is certain is that 'when they had finished everything required by the law of the Lord, they returned to Galilee, to their own town of Nazareth' (Luke 2.39).

As with Matthew, Luke's account of why we have 'Jesus of Nazareth' when he was born in Bethlehem is clear and simple: Jesus' family lived in Nazareth, after which he was named, but were on a short visit to Bethlehem at the time he was born. Again the puzzle is solved.

John, like Mark, has no account of Jesus' birth but brings him directly into the picture when John is baptizing in the Jordan. He also hints at a home-base for Jesus in Capernaum (e.g. John 2.12). More significantly he records two discussions which focus on the fact that Jesus comes from Nazareth/Galilee – and in neither case does anyone have a good word to say for the place.

In the first instance, Philip excitedly tells Nathanael, 'We have found him about whom Moses in the law and also the prophets wrote, Jesus son of Joseph from Nazareth.' To which Nathanael sourly responds, 'Can anything good come out of Nazareth?' (John 1.45–46).

The second discussion relates more directly to our concerns since it also makes specific mention of Bethlehem: 'When they heard these words [of Jesus], some in the crowd said, "This is really the prophet." Others said, "This is the Christ." But some asked, "Surely the Christ does not come from Galilee, does he? Has not the scripture said that the Christ is descended from David and comes from Bethlehem, the village where David lived?"' (John 7.40–42). Further on the chief priests and Pharisees say scathingly, 'Search and you will see that no prophet is to arise from Galilee' (John 7.52).

John differs here from the other three Gospels. Unlike Mark, he appreciates the problem caused to would-be disciples by the fact that Jesus (apparently) does not fulfil the prophecy that Christ should come from Bethlehem. Yet unlike Matthew and Luke, he does nothing to put the record straight, either within the action of the story or in the editorial comments which he makes from time to time in the course of his narrative. There is a puzzle, but it is not solved.

Our four Gospel witnesses all agree that Jesus came from Nazareth. Mark just leaves it at that. He shows no awareness that it might present any hindrance to faith. John knows otherwise. There is a prophecy (Micah 5.2) that Christ is to come from Bethlehem, and the claim that Jesus is the Christ is compromised by the well-known fact that he is a Galilean. But although he is aware of the difficulty, John does nothing to resolve it. Matthew also knows the prophecy – he even quotes it – and he turns it to advantage by telling the story of how Jesus 'of Nazareth' did in fact come from Bethlehem. If that were the end of the matter, we could accept Matthew's version of Jesus' early history without any qualms, although we might still be curious to know why John has withheld this simple solution to his difficulty over the prophecy, and why Mark does not see it as a problem at all. But that is not the end of the matter. There is still Luke's evidence to consider. Luke does not refer explicitly to the Bethlehem prophecy, but he does tell a story which includes Jesus' birth in that town. Unfortunately it is a different story from Matthew's.

Decades of the Festival of Nine Lessons and Carols, whether from King's College, Cambridge, or our local church or chapel, have accustomed us to the notion that there is just one Christmas story, the details of which are divided between two narrators, Matthew and Luke. In the order that the lessons are normally read, first Mary is given the news (Luke 1), then Joseph (Matthew 1); first the shepherds visit the child (Luke 2), then the wise men (Matthew 2); and so on. It is not impossible that such a harmonization of the two accounts does restore to us the historical reality, but if this is the case, then there is a price to be paid. At the very least, there is the matter of omission. Matthew either did not know, or else deliberately chose to leave out, all the material which Luke includes; and vice versa. Perhaps this is not too serious: all biographers have to be selective, and no authors will know everything about their subjects. All the same, it does raise questions about the principles on which the Gospel writers chose their material, and makes us wonder how many other important facts they might have simply have left out or been ignorant of. Second, and more damaging to their status as historians, is one major contradiction. If Luke is right, and the holy family returned to Nazareth six weeks after Jesus' birth (Luke 2.39), then it cannot also be the case that after the birth they fled direct from Bethlehem to Egypt to escape Herod's wrath, as Matthew 2.13–15 records. The two accounts can only be harmonized on the assumption that Mary and Joseph indeed lived at Nazareth, and made a second visit to Bethlehem when the child Jesus was about two years old, during which they entertained the wise men and after which they went to Egypt. Such a reconstruction is not impossible, but it does raise acutely the question of misleading omissions on the part of both writers.

It is important to remind ourselves that these observations all arise from approaching the Gospels as straightforward historical accounts. No 'modern', 'sceptical', or 'scientific' assumptions have been brought in to cast doubt upon the truth of what the evangelists say. It is the Gospel accounts themselves which drive us to ask whether their writers may have had a motive other than just supplying an historical record of Jesus' birth and infancy. To explore what such a motive might be, let us return to the curious attitude we noted in John's Gospel, where the problem of the (apparently unfulfilled) Bethlehem prophecy was noted but not resolved.

One possibility is that John did not himself know where Jesus had been born and that, despite this, he still believed Jesus to be the Christ. An alternative would be that he himself did know of Jesus' origins in Bethlehem, but thought that his readers' faith should not be dependent on this knowledge: rather it should be based on their faithful response to John's record of the signs which Jesus did. We may compare the statement at the end of his Gospel on the reasons for his having written it: 'Now Jesus did many other signs in the presence of his disciples, which are not written in this book. But these are written so that you may come to believe that Jesus is the Christ, the Son of God, and that through believing you may have life in his name' (John 20.30–31). In either case, concern with the fulfilment of prophecy would seem to follow on from faith in Jesus as the Christ, and not be the basis of that faith.

A similar attitude might explain the birth stories in Matthew and Luke. Their contradictions show that they are very unlikely both to be historical eyewitness accounts, but both writers believed passionately that Jesus was the Christ. Both also believed that the Christ must fulfil Micah's prophecy about Bethlehem. So it is fair to say that both of them 'knew' that Jesus must have been born there. God's prophetic word and their own faith in Jesus would together have been stronger evidence than any eyewitness account (or lack of one). And if

9

he was born there, why not say so? Scripture itself would supply the necessary detail.

Supposing that Matthew's story is an historically accurate one, it is not difficult to see how Luke's could have been built up out of a series of Old Testament patterns and prophecies. Any edition of the Bible which has cross-references in the margin will point the way. The name of Gabriel, the angelic messenger, is from Daniel (Daniel 8.16; 9.21); the prophecy of an unlikely birth, made possible by God's power, occurs several times in the Old Testament, for example the promise to Abraham (Genesis 18.10, 14); that Luke had this Genesis story in mind is made more likely by the mention of Abraham in the Magnificat (Luke 1.46–55). This song of Mary's is itself a reworking of Hannah's thanksgiving (1 Samuel 2.1–10). This suggests the idea that Mary is a 'spiritual daughter' of Hannah, just as she was of Abraham. By this we mean that the birth of her son Jesus was a fulfilment of the promise held in the births of Abraham's son Isaac and Hannah's son Samuel. This link with Hannah may also account for the post-biblical tradition that Mary's earthly mother was also named Hannah (Anna or Anne). Bethlehem was, as we have seen, the prophesied birthplace of the Christ (Anointed One). It had also been the home of David, who was summoned from minding the sheep to be anointed by the prophet Samuel (1 Samuel 16.11–13), so what could be more fitting than that shepherds of Bethlehem should be the first to visit the new-born Christ? The visit to Jerusalem for the purification is all of a piece with Luke's emphasis on the piety of his chief characters, and the name of Anna, the devout old woman in the Temple, reinforces the link with Hannah.

If, on the other hand, Luke's is actually an eyewitness version of these events, then Matthew's account is equally explicable as the evangelist's view of what must have happened as the fulfilment of ancient divine promises. Unlike Luke, Matthew often helps us by quoting the texts which have guided him (Isaiah 7.14 for the virgin birth; Micah 5.2 for Bethlehem; Hosea 11.1 for the flight into Egypt; Jeremiah 31.15 for the slaughter of the innocents). Other details are suggested by the connection (via Hosea 11.1) between the story of Jesus and the story of ancient Israel, who by God's design went down to Egypt by the agency of Joseph (Genesis 45.9) and came up again under Moses (Exodus 3.1–12). Like his Old Testament namesake, Matthew's Joseph is a son of Jacob and a dreamer of dreams (Matthew 1.16, 20; 2.13, 19; cf. Genesis 37.1–7), and is noted for chastity (Matthew 1.25; cf. Genesis 39.7–12). From the Moses story come the infant's rescue from child-murder by a tyrannical ruler (Matthew 2.13–18; cf. Exodus 1.22—2.10) and possibly the encounter with magi/magicians (Matthew 2.1–12; cf. Exodus 7). The leading of the star may owe something to the pillar of fire and cloud which led the ancient Israelites in their wanderings (Exodus 13.21) and to the star in Balaam's prophecy (Numbers 24.17 – this text may seem rather obscure to us, but it featured regularly in debates among the Jewish rabbis concerning the coming of the Christ, and the first generation of Christian-Jewish teachers would have been well aware of its significance). The gifts of the wise men, as also their post-biblical status as kings, could be derived from various Old Testament sources (Song of Solomon 3.6; Psalm 72.10, 15; Isaiah 60.3, 6).

What then of us? If, like Matthew and Luke, we believe that Jesus is the Christ, and that Micah's prophecy had to be fulfilled, then we shall believe that Jesus was born in Bethlehem. Whether we accept Luke's version of how it happened, or Matthew's, or both (despite the problems of harmonization), or neither, is of little consequence. Our faith is what counts. If we believe in Jesus but, like Mark and John, are not concerned with demonstrating the fulfilment of Micah, then we may prefer to keep an open mind about where Jesus was actually born. If on the other hand we do not believe in him, then even the equivalent of a birth certificate from the mayor of Bethlehem would be unlikely to persuade us.

For myself, I am happy that Bethlehem should remain the symbolic focal point for 'the hopes and fears of all the years'; but more important than that ancient birth-place is the faith that, here today, 'where meek souls will receive him, still the dear Christ enters in'. That message is the real treasure of the Gospels.

11

2

The baptism of Jesus

Read: Mark 1.9–11; Matthew 3.13–17; Luke 3.21–22;
John 1.29–34; 3.22—4.3

What actually happened when Jesus came to the river Jordan
where John was baptizing? And what did it mean? We shall probably do best to begin on this occasion by reading Mark's account,
because it is the most straightforward. Jesus came from Galilee
and was baptized by John. As he came out of the water, 'he saw
the heavens torn apart and the Spirit descending like a dove on
him' (Mark 1.10). Then came the voice from heaven: 'You are
my beloved Son; with you I am well pleased' (Mark 1.11).

Turning to Matthew, we notice one significant difference: he
tells us that when Jesus came to be baptized, John raised an
objection: 'I need to be baptized by you, and do you come to
me?' (Matthew 3.14). To this Jesus gave a somewhat enigmatic
reply, the precise meaning of which has long been debated by
biblical scholars: 'Let it be so now; for it is proper for us in this
way to fulfil all righteousness' (Matthew 3.15). Other minor differences in wording between Mark's and Matthew's accounts
need not concern us for the present.

At first glance, Luke's account of Jesus' baptism seems closer
to Mark's than to Matthew's. On closer inspection it differs
from both of them in two respects, both of which have the
effect of playing down the importance of John in the whole
episode.

In the first place, Luke moves John into the background by in-
serting a note that John has been imprisoned (Luke 3.19–20)
before he says that Jesus has been baptized. Second, he makes
no specific mention of John in relation to the baptism, which is
itself relegated (grammatically) to a subordinate clause: 'Now
when all the people were baptized, and when Jesus also had
been baptized and was praying' (Luke 3.21). Matthew and

Mark both stress that what follows happened *immediately* Jesus came out of the water. (The word is sometimes lost in modern English translations, but it appears in the original of both Mark and Matthew.) By contrast, in Luke's account it could have happened minutes, hours, or even days afterwards.

With John's Gospel comes the most dramatic deviation from the generally accepted picture. He says nothing about Jesus having been baptized at all, nor about a voice from heaven, but simply has John the Baptist state, 'I saw the Spirit descending from heaven like a dove, and it remained on him. . . . I myself have seen and have testified that this is the Son of God' (John 1.32–34).

Later the evangelist says that Jesus was himself a baptizer of others (John 3.22) – a tradition recorded nowhere else – but he then retracts this statement and says that it was Jesus' disciples who were baptizing (John 4.2). What is all this about? None of the other Gospels makes any mention of even the disciples baptizing people. Only after the events of the first Christian Easter/Pentecost do we hear of Christian baptisms (Acts 2.38).

There is nothing strictly contradictory in these four accounts. Unlike the records of the events surrounding the birth of Jesus, there is no conflicting evidence here to make us question the historical accuracy of any of the evangelists. If we were filming a life of Jesus, it would be quite possible to construct a sequence of scenes which would include all the material contained in the Gospel accounts. Even the confusion over whether Jesus himself actually baptized anyone could easily and plausibly be dealt with. But that is not the end of the matter. Accepting that all the scenes could be historically reliable, the fact remains that by their different selection of material, each of the Gospel writers has managed to convey a quite different picture of what went on. This could be accidental – the result of pure chance and of no significance. On the other hand it might not. The decision to include this or omit that might be a deliberate choice on the part of the author, a choice determined by the true significance of the incident as he understands it and wishes to convey it. If we study such variations only in those cases where internal contradictions force us (historically speaking) to choose between them, we lose an opportunity to build up a rounded picture of each evangelist's vision of Jesus. We also risk missing clues to the wider context in which they were writing, so losing an important dimension of the Gospel treasure. So the baptism accounts deserve a closer look.

Consider the dialogue which raises the question of the relationship between John and Jesus (Matthew 3.14–15). It is the only recorded conversation between these two important religious leaders, yet only Matthew reports it. Why is this? Did the other three evangelists choose to ignore it? If so, it would be helpful to know for what reason they left it out. Or did they not know of it? (Although taking place on a public occasion, the brief exchange of words might not have been heard except by the two themselves.) Or – the possibility has to be considered – is Matthew the only 'witness' to the words because he composed them himself?

The thought of someone making up words and putting them into the mouth of Jesus is not an easy one for most twentieth-century Christians to accept. All biographers and historians have to be selective and leave out some of the available material; they also need from time to time to make editorial comments upon the scenes they describe; but to put such comments into the mouths of the principal characters, as if they had spoken them in the historical situation, would today be regarded as unacceptable. In the case of Jesus, because of the authority traditionally accorded to his utterances, the suggestion is particularly grave. However, if we wish to account for the differences between the four Gospels in relating this event, we ought not to rule out in advance any possible explanation.

There is evidence elsewhere in the New Testament that after both leaders had been executed there was some overlap between early Christians and followers of John the Baptist (see, for instance, Acts 18.24—19.7). It is possible – perhaps even probable – that there was a degree of rivalry between the two groups, which at that stage would both have been movements within Judaism. Disciples of John may well have used the well-known fact of Jesus' baptism by their master to claim seniority for themselves in relation to the Christian apostles. Or it may be that Christian converts were puzzled as to why Jesus (whom they obviously believed to be the superior of the two) should

14

have been baptized by John. Then as now, baptism was probably regarded as a kind of blessing, and – as the Letter to the Hebrews puts it in another context – 'It is beyond dispute that the inferior is blessed by the superior' (Hebrews 7.7). So surely, from a Christian viewpoint, it should have been the other way round: Jesus should have baptized John. Or maybe the belief that Jesus had been sinless from birth (2 Corinthians 5.21; Hebrews 4.15) made it seem unnecessary or even improper that he should have undergone John's baptism for repentance. This is all speculation, but the other evangelists' variations on Mark's bare record would be explained by some such embarrassment.

Matthew, by having the Baptist himself raise the question and Jesus give the reply 'Let it be so now', neatly defused the incident in the sense that he prevented its being used as a weapon in any future rivalry between the two men's followers. The take-home message became: (1) Jesus' own primacy was asserted by John's acknowledgement of it, and (2) by asserting that his own baptism was a temporary expedient, Jesus made it clear that it did not imply any perpetual subordination of his followers to those of John.

For Luke this dialogue was unnecessary, because in his Gospel (unlike Matthew's) Jesus' precedence over John had already been established in a meeting between their mothers before either child was born (Luke 1.41–45). This need not mean, however, that Luke was untroubled by the potential rivalry between the two religious groups. The presence, right there in his opening chapter, of a careful statement of John's lesser status implies that it was a very real concern. So now we have a possible explanation for why he put John into the background in his account of the baptism. Since he did not need the dialogue, better to keep the Baptist well away from centre-stage altogether.

Similar considerations would account for why the Fourth Evangelist went even further and (to be quite safe) removed any reference to Jesus' being baptized at all. John's Gospel, like Matthew's, also has the Baptist make his own clear testimony of his inferiority when he says to his disciples, 'After me comes a man who ranks ahead of me because he was before me. . . . He must increase, but I must decrease' (John 1.30; 3.30).

The differences between the four accounts of the descent of the Spirit may seem trivial, but again they are worth noting for what they might contribute to a fuller picture of each evangelist's particular concerns.

Mark emphasizes Jesus' own experience and records the whole event from his point of view: it is Jesus who sees the heavens torn apart, and the Spirit descend like a dove, and who hears the voice address him personally – 'You are my Son' (Mark 1.11). There is no indication that anyone else was aware of these things.

In Matthew the public side of things is brought out. The opening of the heavens is part of the narrative – not part of Jesus' vision, which is confined to the dove – and the heavenly voice addresses the crowd – 'This is my Son' (Matthew 3.17).

Luke on this occasion both combines elements in the other two and also adds a note of his own. With Matthew he narrates the opening of the heavens, and then includes – as a publicly observed fact – the descent of the Holy Spirit; he even increases the objectivity of the dove by adding 'in bodily form' (Luke 3.21–22). But he agrees with Mark in having Jesus addressed individually. (Some early manuscripts of Luke's Gospel have the alternative wording, 'You are my Son, today I have begotten you.' This is a direct quotation from Psalm 2, which was probably used in ancient Israel on the occasion of the anointing of a new king. It appears at Acts 13.33 with reference to Jesus' resurrection. Whichever wording Luke wrote, the point that it is a personal address to Jesus remains.) Luke also notes that Jesus was praying at the time, and he may have intended this detail to increase further the reader's sense of the subjective element of Jesus' experience.

John's Gospel is again out on its own. Having omitted any reference to the water baptism, the Fourth Evangelist turns the descent of the Spirit/dove into a vision for the Baptist, who only later tells his hearers what he has seen (John 1.32). Similarly, there is no voice from heaven, but the Baptist himself testifies that 'this is the Son of God' (John 1.34).

So what actually happened? Was it an objective event or was it a vision? If it was a vision, was it seen by Jesus only, or by John only, or by the whole crowd? I think the only honest answer is that we cannot tell. And I would add that it is not important. The significance of this part of the story (agreed by all four evangelists) is that it interprets the event as confirming Jesus' identity and empowering him for his mission. That is its significance. That – not the historical detail – is the Gospel truth in relation to this incident.

3

The temptations of Jesus

Read: Matthew 4.1–11; Mark 1.12–13; Luke 4.1–13

The first three Gospels tell us that, after his baptism, the first thing Jesus did under the influence of the Spirit was to undergo a period of about six weeks' temptation (testing) in the wilderness. John makes no mention of this. (This is a typical example of the synoptic Gospels having something in common that John lacks, or lacking something that he includes.)

The shortest account of the temptations is in Mark. He says simply that the Spirit 'drove' (literally 'expelled' or 'threw out') Jesus into the wilderness where three things happened: 'He was in the wilderness for forty days, tempted by Satan; and he was with the wild beasts; and the angels waited on him' (Mark 1.13).

Matthew and Luke both have a longer version of events, much of the extra material being shared, but with differences of detail. To start with, both say that Jesus went without food. (Our familiarity with their longer versions of this story may have caused us to overlook the fact that Mark says nothing about Jesus having fasted during the forty days. We shall return to consider the possible significance of this.) Then each of them details three particular temptations: first to turn stones to bread; next to throw himself off the pinnacle of the temple; and third to worship the devil in return for all the kingdoms of the world and their glory. (This is the sequence in Matthew; Luke has Matthew's second and third temptations in reverse order.) Finally, according to Matthew, 'the devil left him, and suddenly angels came and waited on him' (Matthew 4.11). Luke ends on a more menacing note: 'When the devil had finished every test, he departed from him until an opportune time' (Luke 4.13).

Of all the stories in the Gospels, this perhaps is the one which, even in theory, it would be most difficult to verify historically.

It is an account of Jesus' inner spiritual conflict at a crucial time of his life. He had undergone baptism at the hands of John the Baptist and this is a record of how he responded to that experience and prepared for his own public ministry. It is certainly possible that he afterwards told his disciples of his time in the wilderness and gave the details of his temptations. But in that case we are bound to ask why Mark chose to leave out so much, and why Matthew and Luke could not agree on the order of events. We also need to ask why Jesus chose to share these particular private experiences. There is nothing comparable elsewhere in the Gospels, unless it is his prayer of agony in Gethsemane (Matthew 26.39–40; Mark 14.35–36; Luke 22.41–45) which we shall consider later. Before we can answer such questions, we need to look in more detail at the passages themselves.

'Forty days and forty nights' was a momentous timespan in the biblical narrative: it was the length of time that Moses spent fasting upon Mount Sinai (Horeb) when he received the divine law (Exodus 24.18; Deuteronomy 9.18) and the length of time that Elijah was sustained by the food given him by an angel as he journeyed to Mount Horeb (1 Kings 19.8). By timing Jesus' stay in the wilderness in that precise way, including the words 'and nights', Matthew is encouraging his readers to associate Jesus with these two Old Testament heroes, representative, perhaps, of the Law and Prophets that are to be fulfilled in him. A similar point is made later in all three synoptic Gospels when it is told how Jesus was transfigured in the presence of Peter, James and John and appeared to them speaking with Moses and Elijah (Matthew 17.3; Mark 9.4; Luke 9.30).

At first glance Mark and Luke appear to lessen the impact by speaking simply of 'forty days', but by shortening the familiar formula they may have another purpose in mind: to direct our thoughts not only to the 'forty days and forty nights' but to the equally resonant biblical length of 'forty years'. In particular it was forty years that God sustained Israel as she journeyed after leaving Egypt (Deuteronomy 2.7) and fed her with manna in the wilderness (Exodus 16.35), despite her complaining and putting God to the test at Massah and Meribah (Psalm 95.8–10). We have already seen (p. 10 above) how Matthew applied

Hosea 11.1, 'Out of Egypt I have called my Son', to Jesus. This parallel between the pattern of Jesus' life and that of the Israelites under Moses can fruitfully be followed further. As Israel had passed through the Red Sea and spent forty years led by God in the pillar of cloud and fire in the wilderness of Sinai, so Jesus passed through the waters of the Jordan at his baptism and spent a symbolic forty days led by the Spirit of God in the wilderness of Judea. The crucial difference between the two cases is that whereas Israel of old failed when put to the test (and even put God to the test in return), Jesus came through his temptations with flying colours.

If this seems fanciful, take a further look at the details of the temptations which face Jesus and at the Old Testament texts that he quotes to counter the tempter's arguments. If we think of Jesus' temptations as his personal testimony of his actual experience, then we should imagine these texts going through his mind – as a Jewish boy he would have learned them by heart – as he pondered his future and argued within himself how to respond to the call he felt at his baptism. If, on the other hand, we think that these episodes are more likely to be creations of the evangelists, we should picture the first genera-tion of Christians meditating on the Old Testament Scriptures in the light of their faith in Christ. Like the risen Lord himself in the story of the walk to Emmaus, the Gospel writers (or their predecessors) interpreted those texts as being fulfilled in him (Luke 24.27). That is the approach I shall take in what follows, but the parallels apply just the same if we attribute the accounts to Jesus himself.

We have already noted that Matthew and Luke introduce the idea, absent from Mark, that Jesus went without food during his time in the desert. This might have been an assumption made on the grounds that there is not usually much food avail-able in the wilderness, or it may have been a deduction drawn from the parallels with Moses and Elijah. Whichever it was, lack of food suggested hunger, and hunger suggested the temp-tation for Jesus to turn the loaf-shaped desert stones into actual bread. The two Gospels agree on Jesus' response: 'It is written, "One does not live by bread alone"' (Matthew 4.4; Luke 4.4; quoting Deuteronomy 8.3). Matthew characteristically gives a longer version of the quotation, but the interesting thing from our point of view is where it comes from. It is from the very section of Deuteronomy which describes the Israelites' forty-year wilderness wanderings and God's feeding them with manna. Here is the sentence in its original context:

> Remember the long way that the Lord your God has led you these forty years in the wilderness, in order to humble you, testing you to know what was in your heart, whether or not you would keep his commandments. He humbled you by letting you hunger, then by feeding you with manna, with which neither you nor your ancestors were acquainted, in order to make you understand that one does not live by bread alone, but by every word that comes from the mouth of the Lord. (Deuteronomy 8.2–3)

According to Matthew, the temptation for Jesus to misuse his power in private, by supplying food for his own desire, was followed by the temptation to misuse his power in a very public way – by leaping off the pinnacle of the temple in Jerusalem, secure in the knowledge that, since he was God's son, God's angels would protect him. That might seem to have nothing to do with the wilderness wanderings, but Scripture meditation hardly ever moves in straight lines. The connection becomes clear if we are patient and take things in two stages. First we need to read on in Exodus from chapter 16 (where the Israelites complained of hunger and were fed with manna) to chapter 17, where we find them complaining again, this time that there is no water. At God's command, Moses strikes the rock with his rod and brings forth water, but he is angry with the people for putting God to the test and he names the place Massah (meaning Test) to shame them. Now we turn to Deuteronomy. The whole book of Deuteronomy is a retelling of the story of the wilderness wanderings, already related in Exodus. We find the place we want, referring to the incident of the water, at Deuteronomy 6.16: 'Do not put the Lord your God to the test, as you tested him at Massah.' This is precisely the text quoted by Jesus in Matthew 4.7 (=Luke 4.12) in response to the temptation to jump off the temple roof: 'Do not put the Lord your God to the test.' So we discover that there is, after all, a firm link in the evangelists' minds between this temptation overcome by Jesus, and the shameful time when ancient Israel put God to the test in the desert.

The site of the final temptation in Matthew – a high mountain commanding a view of 'all the kingdoms of the world' – may be an echo of Mount Nebo, where Moses at the end of his life looked out across the Jordan at 'the whole land' which God was giving to his people Israel (Deuteronomy 34.1). But the substance of the temptation – to worship a false God – is an unmistakable reference to that most notorious of all Israel's wilderness rebellions: the worship of the Golden Calf (see Exodus 32). That sin took place under the shadow of Mount Sinai (confusingly named Horeb in Deuteronomy) at the very time when Moses was on the mountain receiving from the Lord their God the 'Ten Commandments', with their opening demand that the Lord's people should worship him alone. The actual text cited by Matthew and Luke as Jesus' response to the temptation is, as usual, from the account in Deuteronomy: 'Worship the Lord your God, and serve only him' (Deuteronomy 6.13).

Whatever exactly happened to Jesus during those weeks immediately following his baptism, the message from Matthew and Luke is clear: in Jesus we have the one in whom Israel's calling to be God's child is fulfilled. He has now succeeded where in the past she failed, but now she also fulfils her destiny because he is himself one of the children of Israel. (Luke rams the latter point home by placing Jesus' family tree between the accounts of his baptism and temptations.) That is the heart of the story: the fulfilment of Israel's vocation and destiny in the person of Jesus. But it is not quite the end of the story. There are still a few more interesting points to extract from Luke and Matthew, and we must also return to Mark, who has so far been disgracefully ignored, to see whether his brief account may not yet have some new treasure to add to what we have aleady mined from the temptation narratives.

First, why the difference in order between Luke and Matthew? If the account in fact goes back to Jesus, then I do not think there is any way of telling which evangelist has the original. But as with the case of the divergent birth narratives, I believe we can explain and make sense of the two versions we have.

Matthew's likely reasoning I have already outlined: the forty-day period in the wilderness setting suggests that the first temptation should be to gratify hunger; the second makes a natural pair to the first (private/public); and the third makes an appropriate climax because it relates to the most serious of all sins: false worship. Luke would not argue with that, but he has another central theme which takes precedence. That is the pivotal role of Jerusalem and its temple in his writing. Luke's Gospel opens in the temple, with Zechariah going about his priestly duties and being accosted by the angel Gabriel, who announces that the old man will be the father of John, who will prepare the way of the Lord. And the final verse of his Gospel reads: 'and they [Jesus' disciples] were continually in the temple blessing God'. In between he is unique both in recounting two early visits by Jesus to the Jerusalem temple, one as an infant of six weeks (Luke 2.22–39) and one as a boy of twelve years (Luke 2.41–51), and also in casting a large section of his Gospel in the form of an extended journey to Jerusalem by Jesus and the disciples (Luke 9.51—19.48). It is Luke alone who records the saying of Jesus that, 'it is impossible for a prophet to be killed away from Jersualem' (Luke 13.33). Given all that emphasis, it is not surprising that Luke should favour the order of the temptations which sets the climax on the pinnacle of the temple in Jerusalem.

Second, a footnote on the 'high mountain' in Matthew. We have just seen that Luke ends both his temptation narrative and his Gospel in the temple. It is interesting to note that Matthew ends both his temptation narrative and his Gospel on a mountain. His Gospel ends with Jesus standing among his disciples on a mountain in Galilee saying, 'All authority in heaven and on earth has been given to me.' It is as if Matthew were saying to us: you see, Jesus ended up gaining in God's way the very thing which he had refused to accept on the tempter's terms.

Third, I said in my introduction that I am fascinated by things that one or another of the Gospels leave unsaid. So I ask myself, why is there no reference in Luke's temptation story to those ministering angels, who feature not only in Matthew, but even in the highly abbreviated account given by Mark? Luke, of all people, is not as a rule squeamish about angels, so there is

23

probably a good reason for their absence here. The reason, I believe, is that he has not omitted the angelic ministry to Jesus but has postponed it. For Matthew and Mark, it would seem, the temptations were a kind of preliminary testing that Jesus needed to get out of the way before he could embark upon the real business of his life. But in Luke they look more like an intrinsic part of the real business of his life. At the Last Supper, Luke alone relates that Jesus said to his disciples, 'You are those who have stood by me in my trials' (Luke 22.28). The Authorized Version renders this 'who have continued with me in my temptations', a translation which brings out even more the sense of continuity between the forty-day period after Jesus' baptism and the time of his public ministry. Then after the supper, when Jesus leads his little band out to the Mount of Olives (Luke does not name Gethsemane, but simply – ominously – calls it 'the place'), Matthew and Mark tell us that Jesus himself prayed; only later, after he had found them asleep, did he command them also, 'Keep awake and pray that you may not come into temptation' (Matthew 26.41; Mark 14.38). Luke alone says that even before he prayed himself, Jesus also told his disciples to pray: 'Pray that you may not come into temptation' (Luke 22.40). Then, crucially, Luke says that 'an angel from heaven appeared to him and gave him strength' (22.43). Some of the earliest, and generally most accurate, manuscripts of Luke do not include this reference to the angel, and a number of scholars therefore doubt its authenticity. I have no doubt (a) that Luke did himself include this verse and (b) that this 'angel of the agony' is his version of the ministering angels in the earlier temptation narratives of Matthew and Mark. For Matthew the arrival of the angels indicated that the time of temptation was over, and the implication is that the angels gave the victorious Jesus a kind of congratulatory party. But for Luke it was not 'all over' at that early stage, because the devil had not been defeated but only beaten off, to await another opportunity. The whole of Jesus' ministry was to be a time of temptation, and the angel who came while Jesus was in anguish of spirit awaiting his arrest was not there to congratulate him on a victory attained but to strengthen him during the last and fiercest time of conflict.

And so to Mark. We have already seen that he makes no reference to fasting, which for his fellow evangelists is essential to make sense of the first temptation, and that he does speak about the presence of wild beasts (to which they make no reference). We normally read his brief account in the light of their longer versions, taking the lack of food as read and the presence of the beasts as a colourful detail that enhances the sense of loneliness and menace in the wilderness. That may be a mistake. In the Old Testament it was God's will that humans and beasts should live peacefully together in harmony. It was how the garden of Eden had been pictured. Adam was never told he could eat meat; that permission only came after Noah's flood (see Genesis 1.29; 2.15–16; 9.1–7). It was also anticipated as one of the hallmarks of God's future reign of peace (see, e.g., Isaiah 11.1–9). Another such sign would be the blossoming of the desert (Isaiah 35.1–2) and the coming of fruitfulness to barren wastes. Maybe, in Mark's mind, the time spent by Jesus in the wilderness after his baptism not only was a period of testing, but also saw the first fulfilling of these prophecies. The descent of the Spirit and the declaration of Jesus' divine sonship allowed, perhaps, a brief foretaste of the future conditions of paradise. This can only be speculation, but I find it a positive and fruitful theme for meditation. It transforms these two verses of Mark's Gospel from a bare précis of an account made familiar elsewhere into a rich source of insight for handling the 'wilderness periods' in our own lives. Gospel treasure indeed.

4

'Your sins are forgiven'

Read: Matthew 9.1–8; Mark 2.1–12; Luke 5.17–26

The tale of 'one sick of the palsy, which was borne of four' (as the Authorized Version memorably put it) is a gift to the dramatic preacher. No healing miracle is more vividly portrayed in the Gospels than the account of this paralysed man who was carried by his four friends and then – in a daring piece of queue-jumping – let down through the roof and deposited at Jesus' feet. The story has been retold a thousand times in sermons and school assemblies, the gathered hearers being invited to relive the drama as it unfolds: to imagine the very roof under which they are now sitting being ripped apart, to feel the alarm and the panic, to see and hear the surprised looks and shouts, the anger of the householder, the calm of Jesus, the suspicion of the scribes, and so on. The scene is unforgettable.

So how did Matthew come to forget it? Or else deliberately leave it out? John does not mention it either, but he omits the entire incident and may have been unaware of it. Matthew, on the other hand, clearly knows about it, because he retains the distinctive debate between Jesus and the scribes, which accompanies this healing in all three synoptic Gospels. Perhaps Matthew was simply running short of space. In my Bible, Mark relates this incident halfway down the second page of his Gospel; Matthew does not reach it until page eight, having had to make room for the whole of the Sermon on the Mount in addition to other material not found in Mark. I do not think we should ignore simple considerations like this when we are trying to puzzle out why the Gospels differ – sometimes we are tempted to look for a deep spiritual reason when a simple practical one may be nearer the mark. However, in this case the space problem is unlikely to be the whole answer, because Luke is also on page eight for this story, and he tells it in full.

Whenever two accounts differ because one is longer, and has detail lacking from the other, the question arises whether the shorter version is an abbreviation, or the longer one has been embroidered. As a general approach in life, I think, we accept the need for trimming detail but we are suspicious of embroidery. We treat creative additions as lies, positive untruths, which rob the enlarged version of the right to be considered a reliable account of the original event. By contrast, knowing what to leave out is considered a legitimate and indeed essential part of the historian's art. If we think about it for a moment, we can see that this is sheer prejudice. It is possible to distort the significance and meaning of an event every bit as much by deletion as by addition. But it is a prejudice nearly everyone shares: not telling the whole truth is widely regarded as less wicked than telling lies. I believe this prejudice may have had an unfortunate effect on our reading of the Gospels.

Since we generally find omission a more acceptable form of varying the truth than addition, and since we believe the Gospels to be essentially (indeed proverbially) true, we tend to assume that the longest version of any story we have about Jesus is going to be the most accurate. We can accept that by ignorance, or by the need to save space, or for some other good cause, the evangelists did from time to time leave things out. We find it almost impossible to imagine them putting things in – that is to say, making them up, and attributing to Jesus words or actions that he did not in fact say or do. Readers who have followed me so far through this series of Bible studies will appreciate why this prejudice makes me uneasy. To recall just one example: Matthew, Luke and John seem all to have felt the need to assert Jesus' superiority over John the Baptist, despite his having submitted to John's baptism. I have suggested that each does this in a different way: Matthew does it by creating a private dialogue between the two leaders; Luke by having a meeting between their pregnant mothers and also by referring to Jesus' baptism only in passing; and John (the Evangelist) by quietly dropping from his account the fact that John (the Baptist) baptized Jesus at all. I think it is arguable that the last of these is the one (so far as we can reconstruct what is likely actually to have happened)

27

that involves the greatest distortion, despite its operating entirely on the principle of omission.

There can be many reasons for adding or altering details when telling a story. One reason is to involve the audience and help them to enter into the scene. If the character 'George' about whom I am talking is known personally to them, then I may well say something like 'You know George – he used to run the village store.' But if George is a total stranger to my hearers, such a reference would be a meaningless distraction and I had much better leave it out. We probably have an example of this kind in the account of Jesus' journey to be crucified. All three synoptics mention Simon of Cyrene as the man forced by the soldiers to help carry Jesus' cross. Mark alone adds that Simon was 'the father of Alexander and Rufus' (Mark 15.21). Today we have not the faintest idea who Alexander and Rufus were, but presumably Mark and his readers did. Matthew and Luke make no mention of them and we may assume that they were as baffled as us by their identity.

Alternatively, extra detail is sometimes needed for the opposite reason, precisely because the audience is not familiar with the characters involved and needs some information to make sense of the story. In the Britain of the 1980s anyone could refer to 'Mrs Thatcher', or to 'Maggie', or even just to 'Her', without saying who they meant. Today, especially for younger listeners, they would need to explain that they were referring to a particularly forceful and reforming right-wing prime minister, etc. etc. An example of the evangelists needing to provide such extra information for their readers may be seen in the case of Barabbas (e.g. Luke 23.18–19).

There is, however, a difference between choosing to include or exclude a particular detail which is in fact historically accurate, and deciding to invent some dialogue or action that had no historical reality. It is this element of invention that makes us uneasy. The dangers of it were humorously exposed by W.S. Gilbert in *The Mikado*. One of the characters, Pooh-Bah, gave a highly colourful 'description' of a totally fictitious event, his purpose being to make the fiction more plausible. When caught out, he excused himself on the grounds that it was,

'Merely corroborative detail, intended to give artistic verisimilitude to an otherwise bald and unconvincing narrative.'

No-one will equate the evangelists with Pooh-Bah. And no-one could call the healing of the paralysed man a 'bald and unconvincing narrative', even in its slimmed-down Matthean version. All the same, the idea that Mark and Luke made up the episode of the letting-down through the roof – rather than that Matthew omitted it – does take some swallowing. Pooh-Bah's outrageous fictions were at least told with the best of intentions: to save a man's life. And we have suggested that Matthew introduced the dialogue between Jesus and John the Baptist in order to safeguard the truth of Jesus' superiority. So a Gospel writer might from time to time embroider the story of the Saviour in order to bring out his message and carry forward the work of salvation. But what truth could possibly be safeguarded by the creative addition of this escapade by the paralysed man's four friends? What honourable purpose could such a fiction serve? Is it not more likely that Matthew deliberately left out the exciting roof-breaking prelude in order to focus more sharply on the real point of this healing miracle – the claim of Jesus to forgive sins?

It is a notable feature of Mark's Gospel that, although the shortest of the four, it tends to have the most detailed and graphic accounts of the episodes it includes. Matthew, although much longer overall, regularly displays the more austere version when they both relate the same incident. He cuts out the circumstantial details and concentrates on the key issue. It is more than likely that this was his reasoning here. The story already has three elements: Jesus' declaration that the man's sins are forgiven, the scribes' questioning of his authority in this regard, and the healing that settles the issue by demonstrating Jesus' power. Matthew may well have felt that it was top-heavy and would be improved by deleting the dramatic introduction. Many a preacher has found the congregation remembering the gripping opening of the sermon but forgetting the final message. Matthew may have sensed the danger of something similar in this case.

Suppose, however, that this was not what happened. Suppose that Matthew's account is more or less the form in which Mark received the story. Can we say anything to explain why he might have gone to the extraordinary lengths of making up the business about the roof? I think we can. Just as Matthew might reasonably have cut out the material in order to focus on Jesus' claim to forgive sins, so Mark might have created the incident with precisely the same purpose in mind.

Among the Jewish leaders of Jesus' time, the priests in Jerusalem belonged to the party of the Sadducees. They did not believe in the resurrection of the dead (Matthew 22.23; Mark 12.18; Luke 20.27) and for them the place where forgiveness of sins was achieved was in the temple at Jerusalem by means of the sacrifices which they offered. By contrast, the local rabbis and scribes in the towns and villages of Galilee would have been Pharisees. They did believe in the resurrection (Acts 23.6–8) and would have looked forward to receiving forgiveness of sins direct from God after their death. As a Christian, Mark would have believed (against the Sadducees) that Jesus had replaced the temple and sacrificial priesthood as the means of obtaining forgiveness and (against the Pharisees) that in Christ divine forgiveness was available here in this life. This second claim was precisely what the argument between Jesus and the scribes centred on in this story. It is possible that Mark decided to bring this out by creating a drama in which a burial is enacted. The paralysed man is carried by four bearers exactly as though he were dead (cf. Luke 7.12–15). His friends then 'dig up' the roof (the word appears only here in the New Testament; its usual meaning is to dig up the ground) and lower him as if for burial. There he meets God in Christ, is forgiven his sins and 'resurrected' to his new life (the same word is used both for 'getting up' from a lying position and for the resurrection of the dead).

One cannot be certain, but on balance I think it likely that the incident actually did happen and that Mark has simply retold it in a way intended to bring out this parallel with a burial. In that case we must assume that Matthew deliberately omitted the incident for the reasons already surmised. Luke recounts the action, but there are many hints in his Gospel that his congregation was more affluent than Mark's. They were probably townsfolk rather than villagers and would have had more substantial houses with stone rather than earth roofs. At all events, Luke speaks of taking up the tiles of the roof, rather than of digging, and he also lacks the reference to four bearers. The combined effect is to lose Mark's funereal overtones without gaining Matthew's crisper focus. For once, Luke does not have the most engaging narrative.

Mark may have had another reason for relating the healing of the paralytic in a way that portrays it as a symbolic raising of the dead. He believed that Jesus was the Christ (the Messiah). We have already seen that his description of Jesus spending forty days in the wilderness with the wild beasts and the angels may reflect his belief that the Messianic Age was already dawning, and that it was being anticipated in Jesus' own life. Among other expected signs of the Messianic Age were the healing of the blind, the deaf, the lame and the dumb (as foretold in Isaiah 35.5–6), and Mark records all these types of healing at Jesus' hands. However, unlike Luke and John, he does not tell of Jesus raising the dead, which under the influence of Isaiah 26.19 had also become part of Messianic expectation (cf. Matthew 11.5; Luke 7.22). So here, and also in the raising of Jairus' daughter in chapter 5 of his Gospel, Mark has symbolic raisings from the dead to make his point. Note that in all three synoptic Gospels Jesus insists that Jairus' daughter is not dead but only sleeping, despite her family's belief to the contrary. Therefore in the evangelists' eyes it is not an actual raising of the dead, such as Matthew 27.52–53, Luke 7.15 and John 11.44, but an actual healing of sickness and a symbolic raising from death.

There is an extreme awkwardness (which has tripped up many a lesson reader) in the way a 'stage direction' is inserted into Jesus' words, first to the scribes and then to the sick man, which is exactly repeated in each of the three Gospels (Matthew 9.6; Mark 2.10–11; Luke 5.24). This closeness of agreement in very unusual wording shows that they must all relate to a single incident, an incident in which the power to forgive sins is the focus of the story. Unusually for accounts of healings, Jesus does not ask the sick person what he wants of him. The man is forgiven 'without the option', as it were, and the implication is that had the scribes not challenged this declaration, then no healing would have followed. The raising up was quite secondary to the forgiving. And this is true of all three accounts. Perhaps Matthew was wise to focus on this key issue, but I hope that, by following Mark's digging up of the roof, we have gained some new insights into the evangelists' methods, and that these will lead us in turn to dig up further treasure from our reading of the Gospels.

5

The parable of the Sower

Read: Matthew 13.1–23; Mark 4.1–20; Luke 8.4–15

The Sower is a parable about the parables. John does not record it, but in the three synoptic Gospels it appears in similar passages consisting of three elements: the parable told in public; a private discussion between Jesus and his disciples concerning the use of parables; and the interpretation of the Sower, also given to the disciples in private.

What is a parable and why did Jesus use them? A common definition of a parable is 'an earthly story with a heavenly meaning' and the reason for their use is generally taken to be the well-tried teaching device of using the familiar to explain the unfamiliar. To put it bluntly, if Jesus wanted to teach Galilean peasants about God, he had to do it by talking about things that Galilean peasants understood: farming, fishing, housework, and so on. At all events, the purpose of these engaging stories is normally assumed to be to help people to understand Jesus' message. We rather take it for granted that he wished to make his audience aware of God's nature and his will for them, to move them to repent of their sins, to seek forgiveness and so to be led to salvation. It therefore comes as something of a shock (to put it mildly) to find Jesus telling the disciples that he uses parables for precisely the opposite reason: in order that people should not understand what he is saying (Matthew 13.13; Luke 8.10) and, at any rate according to Mark, that they should not repent and be forgiven (Mark 4.11–12).

Let us admit at once that there is no easy way to reconcile this astounding statement with the declaration at the beginning of Mark that, 'Jesus came to Galilee, proclaiming the good news of God, and saying, "The time is fulfilled, and the kingdom of God has come near; repent, and believe in the good news."' (Mark 1.14–15). Having said that, however, a closer look at the parallel texts of Matthew and Luke may do something to ease the discomfort caused by Jesus' apparently chilling words in Mark.

Matthew explains the situation as being a fulfilment of the prophecy in Isaiah 6.9–10, which is quoted in full (Matthew 13.14–15). As punctuated in modern English versions, the quotation is put on the lips of Jesus himself. This is a perfectly proper way to read the passage, but if it is correct it must mean either that Matthew added the words to Jesus' reported speech, or that Mark and Luke removed them. However, the Greek original (like the Authorized Version) lacks any punctuation to show who is speaking, so the two verses can also be read as an explanatory comment by the evangelist, inserted into Jesus' words. It is the kind of situation where a modern author would use a footnote, but first-century manuscripts did not have such things. Perhaps we should see Matthew as the forerunner of the editors of the cross-referenced editions of the Bible commonly available today. If the words were indeed added by Matthew (and this point holds whether he intended the quotation to be attributed to Jesus or to himself), then they provide some evidence that he also felt uneasy about the bare words of Jesus as reported by Mark. He seems to have felt that they were in need of some explanation. He found such an explanation in the fact that Jesus' words were a quotation from Isaiah, so he gave the reference and added the longer quotation for good measure.

Luke appears to have handled the situation differently and, we might think, more daringly. There are two separate moves to consider, both of which have parallels elsewhere in his Gospel. We have already seen an example of the first of these in our study of the temptations of Jesus. You may remember how Luke removed the reference to ministering angels from the account of Jesus' forty days in the wilderness, and held it back to use later in the Gospel, during Jesus' agony immediately prior to his arrest and execution (see p. 24 above). A variation on this way of adapting his story was made possible for Luke by his having written a two-volume work, his Gospel and also the Acts of the Apostles (see Luke 1.1–4; Acts 1.1–2). On a number of occasions, if we compare his work with Mark and/ or Matthew, we find that he has left out from his Gospel some detail or verse which they included, only to insert it somewhere in Acts. This may have been one of the ways in which he expressed his belief that in the apostolic church there was a continuation of the teaching and the ministry – and indeed the very life – of the Lord himself. That Luke did believe this about the Church is made clear by the words he reports the Lord as saying to Saul (Paul) during his vision on the road to Damascus (Acts 9.4; 22.7; 26.14): 'Saul, Saul, why are you persecuting me?' (Not 'why are you persecuting my followers?', which was what Saul was outwardly doing.) In the present instance, Luke makes no reference to Isaiah in the Gospel, but at the very end of the Acts of the Apostles (28.26–27) he uses exactly the same quotation, in full, as the final words of Saint Paul in Rome.

Having thus denied himself Matthew's way of defusing the embarrassing words of Jesus reported by Mark, Luke applies an alternative and even more daring strategy. He moves the most difficult clause from the Isaiah quotation ('so that they may not turn again and be forgiven') out of the discussion between Jesus and the disciples altogether and, in a slightly modified form ('so that they may not believe and be saved'), puts it into the interpretation of the parable itself (Luke 8.12). In their new position the words, which in Mark had referred to Jesus' intentions when teaching in parables, are applied instead to the devil's reason for taking the word of God from the hearts of those who have heard it. If this really is what Luke did, it is the boldest example we have seen yet of an evangelist's creative adaptation of Jesus' words. He has not simply omitted or added words, but taken them and moved them, so giving them a quite different significance. One would not attribute such behaviour to a Gospel writer without good reason, but there are two pieces of evidence that support the proposal.

First, we have to account somehow for the differences in wording at this point between the three Gospels. One possibility is that, on different occasions, Jesus himself spoke about his parables in the three slightly different ways recorded by the three evangelists. That Jesus did discuss his teaching methods with his disciples more than once is not in itself unlikely. However, when two very similar scenes are described with small but significant differences of emphasis, one is inclined to attribute the differences to the narrators rather than to a duplicated event. This inclination is strengthened here by the fact that we have seen in the story of the healing of the paralysed man that each evangelist there gives a different version of what must certainly be a single incident (see p. 31 above). If we accept that in the present case also a single occasion is being described by all three evangelists, then if Luke did not change Jesus' words, the other two must have done. And that would leave us claiming that Mark and Matthew put on Jesus' lips the harsh words of Isaiah. I believe it is much easier to understand why Luke might have removed the offensive phrase than why the other two should have added it.

The second piece of evidence comes from another incident where Luke's narrative disagrees with Matthew and Mark. All three Gospels tell how Jesus asked his disciples what people were saying about him, and then asked them who they thought he was, with Peter replying that Jesus was the Christ (Matthew 16.13–16; Mark 8.27–29; Luke 9.18–20). Then all three go on to recount how Jesus told the disciples not to make this information public, and began from this time to teach them how he must suffer and be killed and after three days rise again (Matthew 16.20–21; Mark 8.30–31; Luke 9.21–22). Then comes a divergence. Matthew and Mark both record that Peter rebuked Jesus for speaking in this way and that Jesus in return rebuked Peter, saying, 'Get thee behind me, Satan.' Luke omits altogether this mutual recrimination between the Lord and his leading follower. This is confirmation that Luke is willing to delete offensive words attributed by the other evangelists to Jesus. (If, as in the Authorized Version, the offending words were relocated by the evangelist to Luke 4.8, that would make my present contention even stronger. Unfortunately the manuscripts on which the Authorized Version was based in this instance are now regarded as late and unreliable. The inclusion of the words probably arose from the fact that Matthew has a similar phrase in his parallel account, and a copyist mistakenly added them to Luke to bring the two Gospels into agreement. Such errors frequently occurred when all Bibles were handwritten. Since the words are now regarded as a mistaken addition, they do not appear at Luke 4.8 in more recent English versions and cannot be treated as part of Luke's original text.)

None of this actually answers the crucial question for us: what did Jesus mean by saying that he did not want his words to be understood or to bring his hearers to repentance and salvation? Even if he was quoting Isaiah, it still seems an exceedingly odd attitude to take. At the risk of trying to explain a mystery by a conundrum, I suggest the answer is bound up with the phenomenon known to modern scholars as the 'Messianic Secret'. Several times, especially in Mark's Gospel, we hear that Jesus told those whom he healed not to let anyone know, and that he forbade those who recognized him as the Christ from publicizing the fact (see, e.g., Mark 1.25, 34; 5.43; 7.36; 8.30). By Mark's own admission, the attempt to keep people quiet was a failure. Some cynics have even suggested that Jesus only told people to keep quiet because he knew that the best way to get anything publicized is to say it is a secret. However, serious readers of the New Testament link the Messianic Secret to another matter that puzzled and pained the early Church: why did Jesus' own people reject him instead of recognizing and welcoming their Messiah? The basic answer they came up with was that God himself must have decreed the rejection, chiefly so that time would be made for the Gentiles to be evangelized and brought to saving faith. (The fullest discussion of this is by Paul in the Letter to the Romans, chapters 9—11.) Keeping the secret of Jesus' true identity was seen as part of this divine strategy. Christians also read the whole history of the Old Testament as a long saga of Israelite disobedience and deafness to God's commands, so that their rejection of Jesus was seen as being 'all of a piece' with their past (see, e.g., Acts 7.2–53). The original context of Isaiah 6.9–10 was precisely such a time of Israelite rebellion against God, and the words were given to Isaiah at the time of his call to be a prophet. They were a piece of back-handed encouragement from God to his prophet: the people will refuse to hear you, but it will not be your fault. Now Jesus was giving the same message to his disciples. The context of the Isaiah quotation in Acts 28.26–27, already mentioned above, supports this interpretation.

The parable itself requires little comment. Typically, Mark has the fullest version; Luke, who prefers human interest stories (like the Good Samaritan and the Prodigal Son, which appear only in his Gospel), has the shortest. The interpretation of the parable is clear in general terms. The story refers to the mixed reception that meets the preaching of the Christian message, whether by Jesus himself or by his followers, and gives a word of reassurance to the preacher: just as the sower gets his harvest despite much seed being lost to birds, drought and thorns, so the Christian evangelists will reap their spiritual harvest despite the many who fail to respond with long-term commitment. (In the light of the previous paragraph, we might conclude that the unreceptive soils refer to the Jewish audience and the fruitful soil to the Gentiles.) Nonetheless the parable's interpretation has some interesting variations and confusions in the detail. In particular, there is confusion between the seed and the soil conditions. One expects the seed to represent the preached word of God, and Mark 4.14 and Luke 8.11 confirm this expectation. Then the different types of soil – which are all sown with identical seed – should represent the various kinds of hearers of the word. But this is not what any of the three versions of the interpretation actually says. They all refer to the seed itself (in the different conditions) as representing the different classes of hearer (e.g. 'As for what was sown on the rocky ground, this is the one who hears the word' (Matthew 13.20); 'And others are those sown among thorns: these are the ones who hear the word' (Mark 4.18); 'But as for that in the good soil, these are the ones who, when they hear the word' (Luke 8.15)). This lack of precision seems especially strange in an interpretation that has been 'hyped up' as the blueprint for the understanding of all parables. One possible explanation is that the interpretation originally belonged to a different version of the parable, but that does not explain the confusion within the interpretation itself as to the significance of the seed. My own feeling is that the confusion in the Sower's interpretation is connected with the uncertainty over the purpose of parables expressed in the section we have just finished discussing, which all three Gospels place between the Sower and its interpretation. More than that I cannot say. Here is an unresolved puzzle – a signpost to further treasure? – still awaiting a solution.

Let the last word go to the final verse of the interpretation, where each evangelist puts his own 'spin' on what it means to have the seed grow to harvest in the good soil. For one, 'this is the one who hears the word and understands it' (Matthew 13.23); for another the important thing is that, 'they hear the word and accept it' (Mark 4.20); and for the third, 'these are the ones who, when they hear the word, hold it fast in an honest and good heart ... with patient endurance' (Luke 8.15). These variations, just because they are quite trivial and perhaps almost subconscious, perhaps offer us a glimpse of what each author instinctively felt was the essence of religious practice. For Matthew, understanding is almost a defining characteristic of true discipleship (Matthew 13.51–53). For Luke the quality of perseverance is always highly prized (see, for instance, his addition of the word 'daily' to the injunction to take up one's cross and follow Jesus (Luke 9.23; cf. Matthew 16.24; Mark 8.34)). I have not followed this line of thought before – I am meditating on the passages as I write each chapter, and new insights offer themselves – but I am led to conclude that for Mark it is simple acceptance that matters. I do not think he would have quarrelled with that.

6

The Lord's Prayer (1)

Read: Matthew 6.9–13; Luke 11.2–4

Nothing is more calculated to upset a group of Christians than tampering with the Lord's Prayer. Of all the changes made to our church services over the past thirty years, none has created anything like the resentment caused by changing the traditional wording of the 'Our Father'. So it comes as something of a shock to discover that the 'traditional' wording is not actually in the Bible at all. Matthew 6.9–13 in the Authorized Version comes closest, but even that has the strange 'our debts' where we expect 'our trespasses'. (The first complete English translation of the New Testament, by John Wycliffe in 1380, used 'our debts' in Matthew 6.12, and this lead has been followed by virtually every version since. An exception is the New English Bible, completed in 1970, which gives 'the wrong we have done'. The only example I have found of the word 'trespass' being used at this point is in Tyndale's 1534 translation. It was presumably from here that, a few years later, the wording entered the first English Prayer Book of 1549. And the rest, as they say, is history.) Modern translations omit the familiar ending 'For thine is the kingdom, the power and the glory, for ever [and ever]. Amen' from Matthew 6.13. It is also missing from all versions of Luke 11.2–4, which gives a much abbreviated form of the prayer compared with Matthew. Mark and John appear not to have the prayer at all. So what is going on? Where did the Lord's Prayer come from, and what was its original wording?

The very phrase 'the Lord's Prayer', with the definite article and the capital letters, suggests a single official form of words given to the Church by her Lord. If such an official form of words was given to the disciples during Jesus' earthly ministry, then it is certainly not impossible that it was done in the course

40

of the Sermon on the Mount, exactly as Matthew 6.9–13 records. In that case, however, a very serious question arises as to how and why such a central piece of instruction failed to be recorded accurately in any of the other three Gospels. It is a question that will not go away, and I believe that a careful and honest attempt to answer it can lead to only one conclusion: that at the time the four Gospels were written there was not in existence a single form of words carrying the authority that we now associate with the term 'the Lord's Prayer'.

Although Matthew's is the fullest and most familiar expression of the Lord's Prayer in the Gospels, it does not automatically follow that it is the most original: it may well be that we owe the prayer in its classic form not so much to Jesus as to Matthew. At first encounter that is not a very palatable thought, but consider the alternatives. It is a fact that none of the other Gospels records the prayer in the same words as Matthew does. Therefore if Matthew's full formula does go back to the lips of Jesus himself, then the other three evangelists are guilty on at least one of the following counts: (a) failing to find out about the prayer's existence; or (b) failing to remember accurately the Lord's own words in this important matter; or (c) deliberately leaving out all (or in Luke's case half) of this spiritual jewel. We accept the need for editorial selection, but what kind of a Gospel writer would edit out the Lord's Prayer? I prefer to conclude that the prayer in the form implied by those quotation marks and capital letters was not in fact delivered to the disciples by Jesus during his earthly ministry, but emerged in its full glory only at the end of a process of development that can be traced both within and outside the New Testament.

As mentioned above, the final clause 'For thine is the kingdom, and the power, and the glory, for ever. Amen.' (Matthew 6.13 in the Authorized Version) is not included in most modern translations. This is because it is not found in the earliest or best manuscripts of the Gospel. It is not hard to imagine how this ending came to be added to the prayer. Jewish worship contained many short prayers glorifying God (see, for instance, 1 Chronicles 29.10–11) and these were often added in at the end of other prayers. (A similar thing is found in Christian hymnbooks, where a verse of praise to the Holy Trinity is used, in almost identical words, at the end of many hymns. The Christian use of the 'Glory be' at the end of each psalm during worship is another example.) A short 'praise formula' of this sort, used in worship, is known as a doxology. The familiar ending to the Lord's Prayer almost certainly began life as a doxology added to Matthew's wording in the course of early Christian worship. It would then have found its way into a copy of Matthew's Gospel sometime during the second or third centuries, being added by pious scribes who were familiar with the longer version from their church services, and who assumed that the doxology had been accidentally omitted by an earlier copyist. So the Lord's Prayer 'in its full glory' does not appear anywhere in the original text of the New Testament, not even in Matthew. The first writing that does contain the full version appears to have been the 'Didache', or 'Teaching of the Twelve Apostles'. This short book of Christian instruction is thought to date from about the same time as the four Gospels and it contains a number of passages very close in wording to parts of the Sermon on the Mount (Matthew 5—7), including the Lord's Prayer.

So far this study of the Lord's Prayer has not made comfortable reading. First we have discovered that the prayer in its most familiar English form is not in the Bible at all. Now we are faced with a further unhappy choice, for either one or other of the following conclusions must be true: either (a) even the fullest form of the prayer that we have in the New Testament did not in fact come from the lips of Jesus himself, or else (b) if it did, then it was either lost or ignored by three evangelists out of the four. But that is the extent of the bad news. Now we can turn our energies to a more constructive stage of the process of studying what must be the most familiar few verses in the whole of the Christian Bible. Now we can start to examine in more detail what the Gospels actually say, and begin to appreciate how this living prayer developed and grew among the early Christians.

If we look at all the evidence about the prayer of Jesus in the Gospels, both his teaching about it and his practice of it, there comes over a general sense of prayer as an urgent and intimate pleading with God, as of a child with its parent, rather than a formal recitation of set forms. This, however, is a somewhat one-sided and misleading picture. To start with, it fails to take account of Jesus' weekly attendance at the synagogue, with its set prayer and readings (Luke 4.16). It also leaves out of account the fact that, as a practising Jew, he would have used all the regular daily and occasional prayers which are part and parcel of the Jewish way of life. These would not have been remarked upon because they would have been taken for granted (and shared in) by all his disciples. He did not need to teach these prayers, because everyone in his circle knew them and prayed them, day by day and week by week. The evangelists did not need to record that Jesus used them, because it would never have occurred to anyone that he did not. So these 'routine' private and public set forms of prayer form the essential background to his more spontaneous prayers which, precisely because of their being less common, are the object of comment in the Gospels (e.g. Matthew 11.25–26; Mark 14.35–36; Luke 23.34).

The situation would have changed when the Christian message began to spread outside the Jewish community and to make converts direct from the pagan religions. At this stage there would have been a need for a basic pattern of Christian prayer to replace that provided by the synagogue, and this is just the point in the history of the early Church that the four Gospels were being written. In consequence, it is likely that any tradition of prayer which had been passed down from Jesus was in need of being adapted to meet the new circumstances. In particular, there is likely to have been pressure to provide the kind of prayer formula which was simply not necessary during Jesus' earthly ministry. The very idea of a Lord's Prayer in the sense that we think of it would have been a new one, and this probably explains the lack of consistency among the evangelists in the wording of such a prayer.

I said earlier that Mark's Gospel does not appear to contain the Lord's Prayer. Now that we are thinking less in terms of a set prayer formula given by Jesus, and more of a gradually developing form of words within the life of the Church, it is worth looking again at Mark in a more positive frame of mind. We find that there is in fact a verse which contains an element of

Jesus' teaching on prayer that may have helped to mould both the opening and also the theme of forgiving which is central to the version found in Matthew: '[Jesus answered them,] "Whenever you stand praying, forgive, if you have anything against anyone; so that your Father in heaven may also forgive you your trespasses"' (Mark 11.25). The next verse expands on the need to be forgiving if we are ourselves to receive forgiveness: 'But if you do not forgive, neither will your Father in heaven forgive your trespasses' (Mark 11.26). This sentence is put into the margin of some modern versions of Mark, because there is some doubt about its authenticity. I think it could well be original, but even if it were not, verse 25 alone is sufficient to establish the point I am trying to make; namely, that even though Mark does not give the Lord's Prayer in full, he does record in this single verse two of its key elements. One of these is the phrase '[Y]our Father in heaven'. In Greek, which Matthew and Mark wrote, as in our own English translation, there is only one letter's difference between 'Your Father in heaven' and 'Our Father in heaven'. The other key element is that of mutual forgiveness. This will repay studying in a little more detail.

When two English translations of the Bible use different words at similar places (or even at the same point), this is sometimes because the two translators have chosen different English words to translate a single underlying Greek word. We saw, for example, how John Wycliffe (together with most English translators since, including those responsible for the Authorized Version) used the word 'debts' in Matthew 6.12, while William Tyndale used 'trespasses'. This is simply a preference in the choice of English. At other times, however, the difference in the English corresponds to two different words in the original Greek. Thus the word in Mark 11.25, translated as 'trespasses' in the quotation above, is a quite different Greek word from that used in Matthew 6.12. Tyndale obscured this difference by using 'trespasses' in both places; Wycliffe retained the distinction by using 'debts' at Matthew 6.12 and 'sins' at Mark 11.25; the Authorized Version (and the New Revised Standard Version that I am using) both retain the distinction by using 'debts' at Matthew 6.12 and 'trespasses' at Mark 11.25.

To see where all this is leading, look now at Matthew 6.14–15. Having taken Jesus' teaching about forgiveness at Mark 11.25–26, and made it into part of an actual prayer addressed to God – 'And forgive us ... as we have also forgiven' (Matthew 6.12) – Matthew immediately uses it again, this time keeping it in the form of a warning addressed to the disciples: 'For if you forgive others ... but if you do not forgive others ...' (Matthew 6.14–15). Look to see how the English version you are reading translates these last two verses. In the Greek, Matthew here uses the same word as Mark uses in 11.25–26 (for simplicity let us refer to it as 'trespasses'), which is of course different from the one he had himself used two verses earlier in the Lord's Prayer itself (for simplicity let us refer to it as 'debts'). The kind of detective work we are engaged in – tracing the history of the creation of the Gospel records – requires a translation that does, as far as possible, reflect the variations of the Greek vocabulary. Matthew 6.12, 14–15 and Mark 11.25–26 make quite a good testing-ground for establishing the reliability, in this respect, of your particular translation.

The only teaching of Jesus on prayer preserved by Mark is the piece on forgiveness that we have already quoted. However, this Gospel does record an example of Jesus' own prayer, and that is arguably an even better guide than his teaching about it. So that is where we shall turn our attention next.

I did say at the beginning of this chapter that nothing is more calculated to upset a group of Christians than tampering with the Lord's Prayer. That being so, the investigations of the past few pages are likely to have been hard going, and a break is probably in order to think over what has been discovered. The next chapter will show where the other elements of the prayer are likely to have come from, and why it is still entirely appropriate that we should call it 'the Lord's Prayer'.

7

The Lord's Prayer (2)

Read: Matthew 6.9–13; Luke 11.2–4

At the end of the last chapter I said that Jesus' only teaching on prayer to be passed on by Mark is the piece on forgiveness that we have already studied. However, his Gospel does record an example of Jesus' own prayer, and that is arguably even more important than his teaching about it.

Mark tells us that in Gethsemane, on the night of his betrayal, Jesus had prayed: 'Abba, Father, for you all things are possible; remove this cup from me; yet, not what I want, but what you want' (Mark 14.36). It is more than likely that this has influenced the prayer in Matthew, no less than the teaching at Mark 11.25. In that brief piece of teaching, Jesus had taught his disciples to call God 'Father'. In Gethsemane he was putting his teaching into practice. More than that, he was using the intimate form 'Abba', just as a child would. ('Abba' is an Aramaic word. Aramaic was the everyday language spoken in Palestine at the time of Jesus.) Matthew would have found here confirmation that he was on the right lines when he borrowed the paternal form of address from Mark 11.25. That he kept to the more formal Greek word for father, omitting 'Abba', need not surprise us. Matthew routinely leaves out Mark's Aramaic phrases (other examples are 'Talitha cumi', Mark 5.41, omitted at Matthew 9.25; and 'Ephphatha', Mark 7.34, omitted at Matthew 15.30; Matthew has a general description of many healings at the same point in the narrative where Mark reports the miracle in which this word occurs).

Jesus' plea that he might be spared his cup of suffering (Mark 14.36) was a unique prayer in a unique situation. It would not have been suitable for use in regular corporate worship. (The use of the first person plural in the Lord's Prayer – 'Our Father' rather than 'My Father' – shows that it was intended primarily for corporate rather than individual use.) So that particular cry of anguish did not find a place in Matthew's version of the Lord's Prayer. But the request that God's wishes rather than one's own might be fulfilled (Mark 14.36) was a petition of more general application. Matthew would very likely have thought it an appropriate sentiment to incorporate into his summary or 'blueprint' of Christian prayer, so it was given a place. The addition of the words 'on earth as it is in heaven' was probably Matthew's own idea. He often has the heaven/earth contrast in passages where it is missing from the other Gospels (see Matthew 5.33–35; 6.19–21; 16.19; 18.18; 28.18).

Mark's account of Gethsemane also supplies the petition, 'And do not bring us into temptation' (Matthew 6.13; cf. Mark 14.38). There is, however, a subtle shift in emphasis between the wording in Mark and that in Matthew. In Gethsemane, Jesus had said, 'Keep awake and pray that you may not come into temptation' (Mark 14.38). This sentence has two possible interpretations. On the first it would mean something like this: 'Keep awake and keep busy praying, and that way you will avoid coming into temptation.' In other words, Jesus was giving the disciples two tasks – keeping alert and praying – which together would have had the effect of preventing them from falling into temptation. In fact they failed either to keep awake or to pray, so they did succumb to temptation and all ran away. But that only underlines the point that the purpose of remaining vigilant and prayerful was to avoid that outcome. On this first interpretation the clause 'that you may not come into temptation' gave the reason for praying. Now look again at Matthew 6.13. You can see the change. This is the second way of interpreting the words, and the avoidance of temptation is no longer the purpose of the prayer but its subject matter. It is possible of course to hold both interpretations at the same time, but the introduction of the second possibility is still significant. Once the words 'do not bring us into temptation' become part of the content of the prayer addressed to God, a new idea is born: that God might himself bring us into temptation. After all, it would be pointless to ask God not to do something unless there were a real possibility that he would do it.

We know from the Letter of James that some early Christians

did believe that God himself was capable of tempting them. James would have none of it: 'No one, when tempted, should say, "I am being tempted by God"; for God cannot be tempted by evil and he himself tempts no one; one is tempted by one's own desire, being lured and enticed by it' (James 1.13–14). James has not been alone. Many Christians have been troubled by the implication that God might himself deliberately lead us into temptation. Whenever the Lord's Prayer is discussed in home or parish study groups, it is a subject that always comes up. If Matthew shared this worry – and it is reasonable to assume that he did – then the clause 'but rescue us from evil' (Matthew 6.13) may have been added to the Lord's Prayer by him to address this problem. Matthew might well have felt that a positive request for deliverance from evil would balance and also interpret the prayer borrowed from Gethsemane: our heavenly Father will indeed protect us from the snares of temptation, and he will do it by delivering us from the evil desires which are the true source of that temptation. The word translated 'evil' is a favourite of Matthew's: he uses it 25 times in his Gospel, compared with only two occurrences in Mark and eleven in Luke. It is a word we should expect where Matthew is writing a new phrase and not just copying or recording a tradition he has received. (Crude word-counting of this kind can sometimes be misleading, but it can also be useful as a cross-check when – as here – we suspect on other grounds that a detail, or even a whole passage, may be the evangelist's own creation.)

It has become fashionable for some modern translators to render Matthew 6.13 as 'And do not bring us to the time of trial, but rescue us from the evil one' (New Revised Standard Version). This is a permissible translation, but there are arguments against it on grounds both of original context and of current use. Consider first 'the time of trial'. The great problem here is that hardly anyone knows what it means. Scholars who support this version say that the reference in the prayer is not to those common-or-garden temptations that beset us every day, but to the great time of trial and testing of God's elect that will come before the end of the world. There is no doubt that many – possibly all – early Christians believed that such a time would come, and might well be imminent. Passages in the Gospels (such as Matthew 24.4–36; Mark 13.5–37; Luke 21.8–36) together with various references in the Epistles, not to mention the book of Revelation, bear witness to this. But there is also evidence in the New Testament that leaders of the Church had to curb such speculation and insist upon the importance of ordinary everyday life with its duties and responsibilities (2 Thessalonians 3.6–13 is a classic example of this). It is quite possible, and from what we know of his concerns elsewhere in his Gospel, I should say quite probable, that Matthew originally intended the prayer to refer to everyday temptation and not to that special testing that would be a prelude to the end of the world and the final judgement. And I am even more sure that so far as today's Christians are concerned, what we need and want to pray for is strength to face the stresses and strains and temptations of daily life and to be spared their worst assaults. 'Preserve me from my calling's snare', as Charles Wesley put it, is still a most apt paraphrase of 'do not bring us into temptation' and a most needful prayer for all Christians.

Turning to the choice between 'evil' and 'the evil one' as the interpretation of the final words of the prayer, I suggest that we again take the Letter of James as a guide to how things were viewed at the time the words were written. When James was warning his readers against the idea that it was God who tempted them, we might well have expected him to go on and say something like, 'It is not God who tempts you, it is the evil one, the devil, Satan, etc.' But he does not say this. He says 'one is tempted by one's own desire' (James 1.14). Many Christians down the centuries, from Jesus' own day until ours, have taken that inner source of temptation and projected it on to an external creature – 'the evil one'. They may have been right to do so. But James did not think so, and I suspect that Matthew did not think so either. It is 'the devices and desires our own hearts' that harbour any evil tendencies within us, and it is from them that we need deliverance. So again, on grounds both of original context and current use, the traditional English wording is to be preferred.

It is time to take stock. We are suggesting that 'the Lord's Prayer' in Matthew 6 has been compiled by the evangelist himself. He has constructed it out of originally separate elements of Jesus' teaching and practice of prayer, which he found especially in the Gospel of Mark. He has also added certain explanatory and balancing clauses of his own. So far we have accounted for the following:

(1) Our Father in heaven,
(2) Your will be done,
(3) On earth as it is in heaven.
(4) And forgive us our debts,
(5) As we also have forgiven our debtors.
(6) And do not bring us to temptation,
(7) But rescue us from evil.

Lines 1–2 and 4–6 come more or less direct from Mark's Gospel; lines 3 and 7 can be plausibly explained as additions by Matthew himself. What about the rest of the prayer? Where does that come from? I have already pointed out that, as a practising Jew, Jesus would have used all the regular personal and public prayers required by his religion. His own particular prayers, known to us from the brief references to them in the Gospels, must always be read in the light of that all-embracing tradition of piety within which he stood. Matthew knew this; he knew in particular of the primary duty to keep God's name holy. (Among Jews, no one except the High Priest was even allowed to utter the sacred name of God.) But Matthew also knew that the growing Christian community was attracting many people from outside the strict traditions in which he and Jesus had both been brought up. Such newcomers might well need to be reminded about their duties in respect of the divine Name, especially when they were being encouraged to address God as 'Father'.

We have aleady seen that, unlike Paul (Romans 8.15; Galatians 4.6), Matthew avoided the more familiar term 'Abba', used by Jesus himself at Mark 14.36. I think he would have sympathized with those people today who dislike the use of modern language in church, because it makes us seem too 'matey' with the Almighty. So he certainly avoided 'Abba' and he may have had reservations even about 'Father'. If Matthew did feel a danger in encouraging people to be too familiar with God, then it would make sense if he decided to follow the word 'father' with an immediate reminder of the holiness of God. It would be a wise precaution, and it would not in any way be challenging Jesus' own teaching. Jesus, Matthew would have said, knew very well that God's name should be kept holy. But in these changed circumstances, with all sorts of foreign riff-raff being encouraged into the Church by Paul and his companions, one could not be too careful. One needed to make explicit what previously could have safely been taken for granted. That, I believe, accounts for the insertion of the petition 'hallowed be your name' at Matthew 6.9.

The next line – 'Your kingdom come' – is an adaptation of a very early Christian prayer – Maranatha, Come, Lord! – which is found in 1 Corinthians 16.22 and in Revelation 22.20. The alteration is just what we should expect from Matthew. He would not have thought it necessary to pray for the Lord to come: the Lord had already come and was present wherever two or three of his followers were gathered together in his name (Matthew 18.20). Had he not assured his disciples, 'I am with you always, to the end of the age' (Matthew 28.20)? Matthew was to bring his whole Gospel to a climax with these words. They were central to his whole understanding of who Jesus was: he was Emmanuel, 'God with us', as Matthew had announced in the opening chapter of his Gospel (Matthew 1.23–24, quoting Isaiah 7.14). It is clear from a careful reading of their Gospels that Matthew's understanding of the relationship between the risen Lord Jesus and his Church was quite different from that of Luke. Luke ended his Gospel with Jesus going away from his disciples (Luke 24.51). Matthew ended his Gospel with Jesus promising never to go away. So the prayer for the Lord to come is transformed by Matthew into a prayer for the kingdom of heaven to come. In Matthew's account both John the Baptist and Jesus had opened their ministries with the identical call: 'Repent, for the kingdom of heaven has come near' (Matthew 3.2; 4.17). And it was still coming near. The Lord had come, but his kingdom – his reign in glory – was not yet a reality in the world, so to ask God to bring that about was a fulfilment which could, and indeed should, be prayed for by all his Church.

Only one line of Matthew's prayer has still to be accounted for: 'Give us this day our daily bread' (Matthew 6.11). At one level it needs no explanation. Matthew has recalled by his account of Jesus' temptations how God had fed his people for forty years with the daily provision of 'manna' in the wilderness – just enough for one day, remember, and a double portion before the Sabbath day of rest (Exodus 16.4–35). Matthew had taught his readers, by the example of the Lord himself, that one does not live by bread alone, but he was also to tell them how Jesus fed a hungry crowd of five thousand from just five loaves and a few fishes. So a plea for daily bread to nourish the body made a natural partner to requests for the spiritual blessings of forgiveness and protection from evil.

There is however one curiosity. It is the word translated 'daily'. This occurs only in the Lord's Prayer in the whole of Christian Greek literature and it appears in all three of the earliest versions of the prayer (here at Matthew 6.11; at Luke 11.3; and in the Didache). The earliest translations of the Gospels into languages such as Latin and Syriac, and the earliest commentaries on the Gospels by the first Christian scholars, give a variety of meanings to the word: 'daily', 'continual', 'for our need', 'for tomorrow', 'necessary for existence', 'for today', 'supersubstantial' and 'that comes' have all been recorded. One of the greatest of the early scholars believed the word had been invented by the evangelists to be applied to the bread of the eucharist, but more recently there has been at least one example of its ancient secular use to mean 'daily'. The idea that it refers to the eucharistic bread may however be on target, especially as the divine provision of manna in the wilderness was often treated by Christians as a forerunner of the eucharist. If this is the right interpretation, then it means that all the petitions in the Lord's Prayer are primarily for spiritual rather than for material or physical benefits.

I hope I have given sound reasons to take seriously the likelihood that 'the Lord's Prayer' was composed by the early Church, and in particular by the evangelist Matthew, rather than by Jesus during his earthly ministry. The whole prayer is explicable as Matthew's creation, using ingredients from Mark's record of Jesus' own prayer and teaching. The shorter version of the prayer at Luke 11.2–4 might have been put together by Luke in a similar way, or it might have been shortened by him from Matthew's version. If he believed the prayer really was the definitive model of prayer supplied by Jesus himself, it is very unlikely that Luke would have altered it. But if he knew that Matthew rather than Jesus had compiled the prayer, he would not have hesitated to make his own editorial changes. For example, the bare address, 'Father', rather than 'Father in heaven', would fit in with Luke's account of Jesus' own prayer elsewhere – 'Father, forgive them' (Luke 23.34); 'Father, into your hands I commend my spirit' (Luke 23.46) – prayers of which the other Gospels make no mention. The absence of the prayer altogether from Mark and John, which is very hard to account for if the Lord's Prayer was given in its completed form by Jesus, is also explained by the proposal that Matthew composed it along the lines we have suggested.

Does this mean that we should stop calling it the Lord's Prayer? Not at all. With our modern views we are inclined to draw a much sharper line between the earthly and post-resurrection lives of Jesus than was the case in the New Testament. Living Lord was not a hymn title for the first Christians but a matter-of-fact reality. Paul would quite happily write and tell his churches what 'the Lord' had told him to say about this or that problem that had arisen, and to distinguish this from his own personal opinion. Matthew really did believe that when two or three were gathered together in Jesus' name, the Lord was there with them. So for Matthew it really would have been the Lord's Prayer that he was composing.

Matthew and Paul were not alone in this approach. Holman Hunt's famous painting 'The Light of the World' illustrates the words of Jesus: 'Behold, I stand at the door and knock', but those words are not recorded in any of the Gospels. They are certainly there in the New Testament, but in Revelation 3.20. It is not even claimed that they were spoken by the earthly Jesus, but by the risen Lord through his prophet John the Divine. All the New Testament writers would have thought of themselves as writing under the inspiration of the Holy Spirit and of the risen Lord. That is why modern criteria of 'authenticity' are often not applicable. Jesus spoke through his body the Church just as surely as through his individual earthly body. The Church's prayer was indeed 'the Lord's Prayer'.

8

Feeding the five thousand (1)

Read: Mark 6.35–44; 8.1–10

Right from the very beginning, the feeding of the multitude was one of Jesus' most popular miracles. All four Gospels tell us, with minor variations, how Jesus once fed a crowd of five thousand with a mere five loaves and two fishes (Matthew 14.15–21; Mark 6.35–44; Luke 9.12–17; John 6.1–13). Apart from the events immediately surrounding Jesus' death, there is no incident of comparable length and detail related by all four evangelists. That fact alone would be enough to establish it as a story of great significance to the early Church, but there is more. Matthew and Mark relate that Jesus himself considered the event so important that he repeated it, the second time with a crowd of four thousand, whom he fed with seven loaves and 'a few small fish' (Matthew 15.32–39; Mark 8.1–10).

I am not concerned here with questions of the 'How was it done?' kind. Maybe, as some have suggested, the act of sharing such a small amount of food among so many had the effect of encouraging others to bring into the open their own picnics, which they had been hiding for fear of having the bread snatched out of their hands by hungry neighbours. Or maybe the food just materialized out of thin air: the Gospels resolutely refrain from discussing such details and we could do worse than follow their example. Let us concentrate instead on questions which pose themselves irrespective of the method by which Jesus accomplished the feedings.

First, what are we to make of the claim that Jesus repeated the miracle on a second occasion? Did the second occurrence really take place, or was it just a garbled version of the original feeding that was subsequently, and mistakenly, taken to be a separate event? We have already seen that a single incident in the life of Jesus – his baptism for instance – can be reported by different writers with significant variations. So the possibility has to be considered that this apparent repetition of the feeding miracle can be accounted for in the same way. Even today, with cameras and other sophisticated monitoring equipment to hand, the size of the turn-out at a large march or demonstration can be estimated very differently by, say, the organizers of the event, the police, and the journalists covering the story. So at the time of Jesus, the difference between a crowd of four thousand in one report and five thousand in another presents no serious obstacle to a 'single incident' theory of the origin of the two stories. Also in favour of there having been only one historical feeding miracle is the fact that both Luke and John refer only to the feeding of the five thousand. They might, of course, have known about both events, and quite reasonably decided to save space by omitting the less spectacular one (feeding four thousand with seven loaves and several fish is something of an anti-climax after you have fed five thousand with only five loaves and two fishes). On the other hand, their silence might equally result from the fact that they knew nothing of a second incident, because it had never happened; or even that they had heard about it, but knew that the tale had come about through a mistaken duplication of the original story.

There is also an important detail in the narrative itself which puts a question mark against the historicity of the second occasion. In neither Matthew's nor Mark's account is there any indication that the disciples remembered the earlier miracle. We are told that Jesus expressed his concern for the multitude, because they were hungry and many had come a long way. His disciples' response was to ask, with a kind of helplessness, 'How can one feed these people with bread here in the desert?' (Mark 8.4). Well, the obvious answer to this is, 'The same way as we did it before,' yet no one – neither Jesus nor his companions – makes the slightest reference to any previous feeding. This, to say the least, is odd. Can it really be that the Twelve had forgotten so spectacular a display of their Lord's power and of his compassion? If, however, there had been no earlier miracle, if the two accounts originated in the same single event, then their reaction is perfectly understandable.

So far I have been building a case for treating the two reported feedings as a single historical event, but against this view stands one very significant piece of evidence pointing in the opposite direction. I am not referring now to any of the discrepancies in the numbers of those fed, or of loaves used, or of baskets of fragments left over, but to something much more specific and much more serious. I have said that before the second feeding neither Jesus nor his disciples made any reference to the first one, and that is true, but it is not the case afterwards. Consider the following short passage, which may be unfamiliar (I have never heard it read in church at a Sunday service, whereas the feeding of the multitude – to which it refers – is appointed in the Book of Common Prayer to be read at Communion on no fewer than three Sundays every year). The conversation takes place in a boat on the Sea of Galilee:

> Now the disciples had forgotten to bring any bread; and they had only one loaf with them in the boat. And he [Jesus] cautioned them, saying, 'Watch out – beware of the yeast of the Pharisees and the yeast of Herod.' They said to one another, 'It is because we have no bread.' And becoming aware of it, Jesus said to them, 'Why are you talking about having no bread? Do you still not perceive or understand? Are your hearts hardened? Do you have eyes, and fail to see? Do you have ears, and fail to hear? And do you not remember? When I broke the five loaves for the five thousand, how many baskets full of broken pieces did you collect?' They said to him, 'Twelve.' 'And the seven for the four thousand, how many baskets full of broken pieces did you collect? And they said to him, 'Seven.' Then he said to them, 'Do you not yet understand?' (Mark 8.14–21)

By any reckoning this is a curious conversation and one that is liable to leave the modern reader as perplexed as the disciples. We shall return to some of the details in a moment, but for the present we need simply to note this one fact: Jesus' questions only make sense if there were indeed two separate feedings as Mark has reported. So if the conversation in the boat is historical, there must have been two feedings; and if there were two feedings, the disciples' amnesia on the second occasion has to be accounted for. On the other hand, if there was in fact only one miracle, then Mark (or some earlier tradition on which he was drawing) has not only created two accounts out of one event, but has gone on to produce in addition an obscure piece of dialogue whose meaning was unclear to the characters involved in it and which continues to puzzle readers of the Gospels to this day. This paradox has nothing to do with whether we believe the miracle was a supernatural event or whether it had a natural explanation. It is a problem embedded firmly in the narrative of Mark's Gospel itself (and also, as we shall see, in Matthew's), and there is no simple solution for either the trusting believer or the hardened sceptic.

We can hardly overestimate the importance of all this for our search after the motives of the evangelists and the nature of the truth they proclaim. More than any of the texts we have considered so far, this conundrum puts a question mark against our initial concept of the Gospels as straightforward eyewitness accounts. Inconsistencies in the birth narratives might, after all, be tolerated on the grounds that it all happened long before the Gospels were written. Genuine eyewitnesses may well not have been available. Again, Jesus' response to his special calling, witnessed in his baptism and temptations, was – it might be argued – essentially a personal matter. So it was only to be expected that his attempts to share the experience with others, and their attempts to comprehend and express what had been shared, would result in a confused picture. And those variations in the disciples' recollections of Jesus' healings and teaching – even his teaching on prayer – might also perhaps be accounted for without affecting the principle of the evangelists as the passers-on of historically reliable accounts. But this case is different. If, on the one hand, there was only one historical feeding, then creative writing by Matthew and Mark on a significant scale is the only way to account for the words that appear in their Gospels. That would not necessarily be a disastrous conclusion for us to draw, as I hope to demonstrate. But it would put an end once and for all to the notion that the evangelists were mere passive chroniclers of events. On the other hand, if there were in fact two historical feedings as Matthew and Mark relate, then the record of the second one does raise very serious questions about the disciples' memories and about their attitude and response to the things that Jesus said and did.

Space here precludes a detailed study of the six accounts of the miracle(s). Readers can make the comparisons for themselves and will find the kinds of differences that our previous studies have highlighted. For example, Matthew's habit of giving a shorter account of an incident than Mark (to which I drew attention on page 29 above) is again borne out by a rough count: Matthew tells the feeding of the five thousand in seven verses against Mark's ten (Matthew 14.15–21; Mark 6.35–44), and the story of the four thousand in eight verses against Mark's ten (Matthew 15.32–39; Mark 8.1–10). Noticing this sort of thing soon becomes second nature, and it all helps to build up a feel for the style and even the personality of the individual evangelists. And that in turn helps us to hear and respond to their message.

The question I wish to pursue now is why the feeding miracle was so important to the early Church. To answer this we shall look first at John's account. This will lead us back to the curious conversation in the boat, quoted above, and so by degrees to a possible solution to the earlier question of why Matthew and Mark report two miraculous feedings while Luke and John mention only the one.

John structures his Gospel differently from that of the synoptics. They record collections of Jesus' parables and other short pieces of teaching, interspersed with examples of his miracles; John tends to give Jesus' teaching in the form of long discourses and dialogues on themes provided by particular incidents, or 'signs' as he calls them. An excellent example of this is found in chapter 6, which opens with the feeding of the five thousand (John 6.1–14), and is then largely given over (John 6.22–71) to an extended discussion on the theme of bread between Jesus and 'the crowd' (e.g. John 6.24–25), 'the Jews' (e.g. John 6.41) and 'his disciples' (e.g. John 6.60; these include but are not limited to 'the Twelve', e.g. John 6.66–67). Central to the argument is Jesus' repeated claim, 'I am the bread of life' (John 6.35, 48). The second time Jesus says this he goes on:

I am the bread of life. Your ancestors ate the manna in the wilderness and they died. This is the bread that comes down from heaven, so that one may eat of it and not die. I am the living bread that came down from heaven. Whoever eats of this bread will live for ever; and the bread that I will give for the life of the world is my flesh. (John 6.48–51)

Talk about Gospel treasure – there is enough here to fill Aladdin's cave! – but let us be content with noting just two points. First, we are back with the theme of Moses and the manna in the wilderness, which has already featured in our discussions of the temptation story and of the Lord's Prayer. Here, then, is one reason why the feeding miracle was so important to the early Christians: it formed a central part of the all-important patterning of the life of both Jesus and the Church on the blueprint of ancient Israel. In olden times God had fed his people miraculously through his servant Moses; now he had done it through his Son Jesus. Second, there is a clear reference here to the eucharist, with Jesus equating the eating of bread with the eating of his own flesh. In his account of the Last Supper (John 13—17), John does not make any reference to the institution of the eucharist, such as we find in the synoptics (Matthew 26.26–29; Mark 14.22–25; Luke 22.15–20). His equivalent teaching is here in chapter 6, and it is directly linked to the feeding of the five thousand by the expression in John 6.23: 'the place where they had eaten the bread after the Lord had given thanks'. (The Greek word for 'thanks' here is 'eucharist' and the word-order in Greek places it next to the word for bread. So an interpretation along the lines of 'the place where they ate the Lord's eucharistic bread', while not a strictly accurate translation, restores an important element of the flavour of John's original, which is lacking from the usual English versions.) So now we have the second reason for the central importance of the feeding story to the early Church: it not only looked back to the ancient miraculous feeding of God's people with heavenly manna; even more significantly it pointed forward to God's contemporary miraculous feeding of his people with the spiritual food of the eucharist, Christ himself.

We now have the keys to go back and unlock the treasure-house of the feeding of the multitude as told in the other three Gospels: the manna and the eucharist. This we shall do in the next chapter.

9

Feeding the five thousand (2)

In this chapter we shall first of all follow up the suggestion that the significance of the feeding miracle for the early Church lay largely in its symbolic importance as a foreshadowing of the eucharist. Look again at the six accounts of the feeding of the multitude, especially at the point where Jesus takes the bread (Matthew 14.19; 15.36; Mark 6.41; 8.6; Luke 9.16; John 6.11). Compare the wording in these verses with his taking of the bread at the Last Supper (Matthew 26.26; Mark 14.22; Luke 22.19; compare also Paul's account at 1 Corinthians 11.23–24). There is considerable variety in wording among the different accounts of the Last Supper, but the similarity in general with the feeding miracle stories is unmistakable.

Two things might be felt to tell against the close association I am claiming between the feedings and the eucharist. The first is a matter of words. We were first put on to this tack by John's use of the word 'eucharist' in connection with the bread used by Jesus to feed the five thousand (John 6.23). The word is usually translated into English as 'gave thanks' and it was also used by John to describe what Jesus had done when he took the bread before distributing it (John 6.11). But all three synoptics, when they tell of the feeding of the five thousand, use a different word at this point, normally translated into English as 'blessed' (Matthew 14.19; Mark 6.41; Luke 9.16). Yet in their recording of the second miracle, the feeding of the four thousand, Matthew and Mark both use the 'eucharist' word, 'and after giving thanks he broke them' (Matthew 15.36; Mark 8.6). Just to complete the confusion, in their accounts of the Last Supper, at the institution of what came to be called 'the eucharist', Matthew and Mark say that Jesus 'blessed' the bread (Matthew 26.26; Mark 14.22) while Luke, in agreement with

Paul, says that he 'gave thanks' (Luke 22.19; 1 Corinthians 11.24).

These differences are not in fact too serious – the very way in which the two expressions are so mixed up is evidence that their meanings and use were much more similar than their English equivalents might suggest. We tend to think of 'giving thanks' as something we do to people (in response to some kindness shown to us) and of 'blessing' as something that is done to things, either as a solemn and religious way of wishing them protection and good fortune (e.g. houses, marriages, even battleships), or else to set them apart for a special holy use (e.g. holy water, devotional pictures, crucifixes, etc.). That was not a distinction that the biblical writers would have recognized. For them, to bless something was precisely to give thanks to God for it. So to give a blessing and to give thanks (to God) were identical activities.

The second possible objection to linking the feedings to the eucharist is that the former consisted in each case of bread and fish, while the essentials for the latter are bread and wine. There are several points that can be made here. None of them by itself is conclusive, but taken together they serve to lessen the force of this difficulty. The first is to say that in early references to the eucharist, the bread seems always to have been the more significant element. This is especially true of Luke. In the Acts of the Apostles he several times refers to Christians 'breaking bread' in a way that suggests more than simply 'eating' and that very likely refers to the eucharist (Acts 2.42, 46; 20.7, 11). There is also one place in Acts where Paul, using bread only, goes through actions and words reminiscent of both the feedings and the Last Supper: 'After he had said this, he took bread; and giving thanks [eucharist] to God in the presence of all, he broke it and began to eat' (Acts 27.35). And in his Gospel, at the meal at Emmaus, Luke refers only to bread when he writes, in words that by now are very familiar to us, that, 'When he [Jesus] was at table with them, he took bread, blessed and broke it, and gave it to them' (Luke 24.30). And in telling how Cleopas and his companion reported this incident to the disciples in Jerusalem, Luke again uses the expression 'in the breaking of the bread' (Luke 24.35).

If we turn again to John's Gospel, the absence of wine at the miraculous feeding is more than made up for by the very first of the 'signs' by which – according to John – Jesus revealed his glory: the wedding at Cana (John 2.1–11). In the story of the wedding feast, Jesus provides abundant wine; in the feeding of the five thousand he provides abundant bread; and the evangelist links both incidents to the Last Supper and the death of Jesus by noting in each case that it was Passover time (John 2.13; 6.4; 13.1; 19.14). There is also in John's account of the Last Supper the saying of Jesus, 'I am the true vine' (John 15.1), which parallels the earlier 'I am the bread of life' (John 6.35, 48). It is possible that John's failure to record the second feeding miracle reflects the fact that in the wedding feast at Cana he already has a 'eucharistic' story to make a 'pair' with the multiplication of the loaves. A further clue that John intends the bread of the feeding of the five thousand to represent the eucharistic bread (i.e. Jesus' body) might be found in the curious detail that of all six accounts of the feeding of the multitude, John's is the only one that does not specifically say that Jesus broke the bread before distributing it. And if we turn to John's account of the death of Jesus, he is the only one of the four evangelists to make a specific point of the fact that Jesus' body was not broken, and to tell his readers that this was no accident but rather that, 'These things occurred so that the scripture might be fulfilled, "None of his bones shall be broken" ' (John 19.36). And if there should be any doubt that the wedding at Cana was intended by John to be read in the context of Jesus' death and resurrection, we have (in addition to the reference to Passover) the opening words of the story sounding out like an Easter fanfare: 'On the third day' (John 2.1).

So much for the wine. What about the fish? The clue here lies chiefly in the visual arts rather than the Scriptures. In the first place, the fish symbol was used as an early Christian secret code (the letters of the Greek word for fish being the initial letters of the phrase 'Jesus Christ God's Son Saviour'). It is likely that the fish symbol is being used by far more Christians at the turn of the third millennium than ever were using it in the opening century of the first but, even so, this association of Christ with the fish may be linked to an early use of fish alongside bread as a token of his sacramental presence with his Church. More secure evidence is supplied by wall paintings in the Roman catacombs. The catacomb of Saint Callistus, over a thousand years before Leonardo, has 'Last Supper'-style groups of figures sitting at table with two platters, each bearing a fish, and a row of large baskets over-brimming with bread. Another part of the mural shows a single fish with a basket and a platter containing five loaves. There is not a flagon or chalice of wine in sight. The official 'Pontificia Commissione di Archeologia Sacra' – not a body one would expect to go in for wild speculation – has no hesitation in describing these paintings as 'eucharistic representations'. Whether the pictures are intended to represent Jesus and his disciples, or simply the Roman Christian congregation gathered for holy communion, the link between bread, fish and the eucharist in the third century seems to be established.

Having explored the foreward link between the feeding miracles and the eucharist, we now consider the retrospective connection with the miraculous provision of food in the Old Testament. Pride of place must go to God's gift to the ancient Israelites of manna in the wilderness in the days of Moses, but, before considering that, it is worth mentioning two passages in 2 Kings 4 that prefigure the feeding miracles. Both concern the prophet Elisha and the multiplication of quantities of produce. In the first, he enabled a widow to pay her debts, and make enough money to live on, by enabling her to pour out of her last jar of oil a far greater volume of the liquid than ever it could have held (2 Kings 4.1–7). In the second, he fed a hundred men with a mere twenty barley loaves and some fresh ears of grain, prophesying that there would be food left over, which there was (2 Kings 4.42–44). This pair of stories is especially reminiscent of John's pairing of the wedding at Cana and the feeding of the five thousand. The note that the loaves were of barley is also peculiar to John. These Elisha stories may well have influenced the telling of how Jesus miraculously multiplied food and drink, though the disparity in the numbers of loaves and those fed is, of course, much more marked in the Gospel account than in 2 Kings.

It is now time to look at the link between the feedings by Jesus and the miraculous feedings of the multitude of ancient

Israelites with manna in the wilderness (Exodus 16). If the manna foreshadowed Jesus' miracle, which in turn foreshadowed the eucharist, then the manna also foreshadowed the eucharist, in the eyes of the evangelists and the early Church. And the eucharist was one of the two great sacraments of the Church, the other being baptism. Now the event in the life of the Israelites that immediately preceded their wilderness wanderings was the crossing of the Red Sea (Exodus 14). A somewhat obscure passage of Paul in 1 Corinthians, whatever its precise meaning, points strongly to a link between ancient Israel's passing through waters of the Red Sea and the Christian's passing through the waters of baptism:

> I do not want you to be unaware, brothers and sisters, that our ancestors were all under the cloud, and all passed through the sea, and all were baptized into Moses in the cloud and in the sea, and all ate the same spiritual food, and all drank the same spiritual drink. For they drank from the spiritual rock that followed them, and the rock was Christ. (1 Corinthians 10.1–4)

There is no evidence, apart from this passage itself, of the crossing the Red Sea by the Israelites ever having been referred to as 'baptism'. We therefore conclude that Paul introduced the word in order to make the point that he regarded the Red Sea crossing as a foreshadowing of Christian baptism. We have already seen that Jesus' forty days in the wilderness, following his own baptism, were seen by the evangelists as a fulfilment of Israel's forty years in the wilderness (p. 19 above). So the patterning – the foreshadowing and fulfilment – is all of a piece. That Paul also saw the feeding with manna ('and all ate the same spiritual food') as foreshadowing the eucharist is very likely. The passage just quoted is followed immediately by a comparison between the rebellion of the Israelites in the wilderness and the failings of Christians under temptation, and then comes the following pronouncement, in which Paul clearly refers to the eucharist: 'The cup of blessing that we bless, is it not a sharing in the blood of Christ? The bread that we break, is it not a sharing in the body of Christ? Because there is one bread, we who are many are one body, for we all partake of the one bread' (1 Corinthians 10.16–17). So we find two sacraments for the price of one: Red Sea and manna represent and foreshadow Christian baptism and eucharist. It would complete the circle wonderfully if the feeding of the five thousand in the Gospels were immediately preceded by a story about crossing the water, a story that could symbolically represent baptism. Unfortunately it isn't. But it is followed by one, which is almost as good.

Look again at John 6. Between the feeding of the five thousand (verses 1–14) and the lengthy discussions on the theme of bread (verses 22–71) there is a short section that I have so far carefully avoided. It tells of a crossing of the water – a symbolic baptism, if you will – in which the terrified disciples, alone in the boat with adverse winds, are rescued by Jesus coming to them across the lake (John 6.16–21). John could not reverse the orders of the feeding and the water-crossing – the tradition for the order he gives was presumably too strong – but he did the next best thing by putting his discussion of the feeding, and its specific references to the manna (John 6.31), after the crossing of the lake. So the correct sequence of Red Sea–manna, baptism–eucharist, was in a sense restored.

Now look at the feeding of the five thousand in the synoptics: Matthew and Mark, like John, both follow it immediately with the story of Jesus walking on the water (Matthew 14.22–32; Mark 6.45–51). Luke lacks this incident, together with everything else in Matthew 14.22—16.12 (parallel to Mark 6.45—8.26), apart from a few verses that he has in other contexts. We shall therefore ignore him for the moment and concentrate on Matthew and Mark. Following the walking on the water, they both have a roughly similar series of healings and teaching by Jesus, leading eventually to the feeding of the four thousand (Matthew 15.32–39; Mark 8.1–10). Then, after a few verses of Jesus arguing with the Pharisees about whether or not he will show them a sign from heaven, the pattern of feeding–water-crossing reasserts itself in Mark, and we find the disciples back in the boat crossing the lake and being cross-examined by Jesus. The passage is important enough to print out again:

Now the disciples had forgotten to bring any bread; and they had only one loaf with them in the boat. And he [Jesus] cautioned them, saying, 'Watch out – beware of the yeast of the Pharisees and the yeast of Herod.' They said to one another, 'It is because we have no bread.' And becoming aware of it, Jesus said to them, 'Why are you talking about having no bread? Do you still not perceive or understand? Are your hearts hardened? Do you have eyes, and fail to see? Do you have ears, and fail to hear? And do you not remember? When I broke the five loaves for the five thousand, how many baskets full of broken pieces did you collect?' They said to him, 'Twelve.' 'And the seven for the four thousand, how many baskets full of broken pieces did you collect? And they said to him, 'Seven.' Then he said to them, 'Do you not yet understand?' (Mark 8.14–21)

What immediately strikes me, looking at it a second time, is how similar this particular passage is to that earlier, equally puzzling conversation that Jesus had with his disciples over the use of parables:

And he said to them, 'To you has been given the secret of the kingdom of God, but for those outside everything comes in parables; in order that "they may indeed look, but not perceive, and may indeed listen, but not understand; . . .".' And he said to them, 'Do you not understand this parable? Then how will you understand all the parables?' (Mark 4.11–13)

The repeated themes of seeing and hearing without understanding come over very powerfully. Perhaps it is not just coincidence that these two similar questioning-sessions of Jesus come where they do: one after the parable concerning the multiplication of grain – 'Other seed fell into good soil and brought forth grain, growing up and increasing and yielding thirty and sixty and a hundredfold' (Mark 4.8) – and the other after the miracle of the multiplication of grain-made-bread. Perhaps there is yet more to be gleaned from this parallel between the parable of the seed and the miracle of the loaves. If you have begun to catch the spirit of the kind of Bible-study we are engaged in, it will come as little surprise to you that when we turn back to Mark 4 we find that the setting of the parable of the sower was 'beside the lake' (Mark 4.1) and that once the teaching session was over 'he [Jesus] said to them, "Let us go across to the other side."' (Mark 4.35). What follows is the story of the stilling of the storm. So with hindsight we can see that, for Mark at least, the parable is also a part of the baptism/eucharist patterning, and the sower is a minister of both word and sacrament. (Matthew and Luke both have the story of the stilling of the storm as well, but in contexts which do not underline the pattern that Mark has.)

But we digress. Look again at the questions Jesus asked in the boat. He did not ask about the numbers fed, nor about the numbers of loaves used, but about the numbers of baskets left over. They were the two numbers that the disciples were supposed to 'understand'. And those numbers were twelve and seven. When it comes to numbers in the Bible, there are only two certain things: first, that they are always significant; and second, that no-one will be able to agree as to what that significance is. However, in this case the matter is fairly straightforward. Twelve is about the safest number to interpret: it always signifies Israel. Seven is trickier. Normally it signifies completeness and rest (creation was completed with God's resting on the seventh day, Genesis 2.2): it is the full week. It is not impossible that this is the intended meaning here, but there is an alternative and, I think, more likely interpretation. Biblical writers will sometimes use significant numbers in multiples of ten. For example, at the beginning of the Acts of the Apostles, the small company of believers was, in Luke's eyes, the faithful core of Israel, and therefore ought, symbolically, to have been twelve in number. But that 'twelve' symbolism had already been used for the apostles, and so he gave the number of the faithful as 120 – ten times twelve (Acts 1.15). I believe that, in a similar way, the seven baskets left over from the second feeding stand symbolically for seventy. Seventy was traditionally held to be the total number of nations in the world, so seventy can represent the whole of the Gentile world just as twelve represents Israel.

Twelve and seven(ty) make a natural pairing, as Luke knew when he recorded two evangelistic missions by Jesus' disciples. The first consisted of twelve missionaries (Luke 9.1–10) and took place immediately after the double healing story of Jairus' twelve-year-old daughter and the woman who had suffered haemorrhages for twelve years (Luke 8.40–56). Three twelves in three consecutive episodes is Luke's very insistent way of saying 'This section is about the conversion of Israel'. It closes with Jesus retiring with his disciples to 'a city called Bethsaida' (Luke 9.10). The second missionary journey – the symbolic Gentile mission – had seventy participants (Luke 10.1–17) and is recorded alongside Jesus' cursing of the Israelite towns that have rejected him – including Bethsaida (Luke 10.13).

If I am on the right lines, then the thing that Jesus is trying to get his disciples to 'understand' about the two feedings is that one represents the conversion of Israel and the other the conversion of the Gentiles. Matthew failed to understand this and, in his version of the conversation following the feedings, fell back on the true – but for this purpose irrelevant – point that Jesus used 'yeast' as a code word for the Pharisees' unacceptable teaching (Matthew 16.5–12). Luke, I believe, did get the message, but deliberately dropped it. As we have seen before, he will sometimes leave something out where Mark and/or Matthew include it, in order to use it later on in either his Gospel or Acts. In this case he covers the Gentile angle with his 'mission of the seventy' (Luke 10), so he can afford to drop the second (symbolically 'Gentile') feeding and the dialogue in the boat that relates to it. He prefers in any case to keep the Gentiles at arm's length in his Gospel, because he will be devoting the best part of the Acts of the Apostles to their evangelization. He is happy to drop the second storm on the lake story (with Jesus walking on the water) for a similar reason: he has in store the tale of Paul's shipwreck (Acts 27.13–44), which is a storm story to outmatch anything anywhere else in the Bible (even Jonah).

I believe we have now accounted satisfactorily for the importance of the feeding stories and the reason why John and Luke have only one where Matthew and Mark have two. The discussion has taken us far away from the accounts themselves, and given a good example of the essential interrelatedness of so much of Scripture. As to whether there were originally one or two such feedings, I leave readers to decide for themselves.

10

The Good Samaritan

Read: Luke 10.25–37

Is the story of the Good Samaritan true? That might seem a surprising question to ask. It invites the immediate response, 'Of course it's true! How could a story told by Jesus not be true?' Perhaps that is a better way of putting the question: how could such a story not be true? Or better still – if we are taking it for granted that the story is true – in what sense is it true?

To answer this question, we need to consider whether we are concerned only with the origins of the story, or with its history. That is to say, whether it makes any difference to the nature of the 'truth' of the story that the Good Samaritan is now one of the best-known characters in the Gospels. His name has become synonymous with non-judgemental caring for those in need, especially those in despair, and is known to thousands who have never read it in the Bible. And his story has contributed to the English language not only the word Samaritan itself (in that caring sense), but also the phrase 'pass by on the other side' (to describe the opposite attitude, of uncaring avoidance). In other words, the story has had a long and creative history since it first found its way into Luke's Gospel. So, given all this development, what does it mean to say that the story of the Good Samaritan is a true story? That is the question that will occupy us in this chapter, and a very searching and far-reaching question it will prove to be.

The first and straightforward sense in which the story could be true is that the events on the Jerusalem to Jericho road happened exactly as reported. There is nothing in the text to suggest that Jesus did not relate an historical incident which had recently occurred. The locations, the characters, their behaviour – all are completely credible. Some of Jesus' stories undoubtedly have a 'once upon a time' quality, with over-the-top characters (like the king who burnt down an entire city because its leading citizens refused a wedding invitation – see Matthew 22.2–7), but the Good Samaritan is not one of those. It is a perfectly plausible real-life account which could well have happened. If it did, it would not have been the first or the last time that a teacher has drawn upon a familiar local incident to illustrate and press home a lesson. There is certainly no reason to rule out the possibility that the story was true in that matter-of-fact historical sense. But that is not the end of the matter. The historically true story would still have gained a kind of 'added truth' by the use subsequently made of it to teach a moral truth about loving one's neighbour.

Now let us suppose, for argument's sake, that the story was not true in that historical sense. Suppose that Jesus made it up on the spur of the moment as a dramatic and memorable answer to the lawyer's question, 'And who is my neighbour?' Would that mean that the story was not true in any sense? Surely not. The novels of Charles Dickens were all fictional, but they give us a more accurate picture of life for the deprived and struggling classes in early Victorian London than any number of official reports could do. In that sense Dickens's books are true: they are 'true to life', as we say, and they do convey – through the lives and deaths of characters created by the novelist – the truth about conditions in many schools, workhouses, back streets and slums in mid-nineteenth-century Britain. Similarly, the stories of Jesus may be true without being records of actual historical people and events.

One way in which such parables may be true without being historical is by symbolizing something else, especially the nature of God and his dealings with the world and with humankind. A story intended to be 'decoded' in this way is called an allegory, and in some instances the Gospels themselves give us this kind of interpretation alongside the story concerned. The parable of the sower is one such example (discussed above, see pp. 38–39). The parable of the fishing net (Matthew 13.47–50) is another. The Good Samaritan does not have an explanation of this kind attached to it in Luke's Gospel, but this has not prevented Christian preachers from finding an allegorical message in it. The flavour of such interpretations, which were especially popular from the fourth century through to the fifteenth, can be gathered from the example summarized in the next paragraph.

The story is a symbolic representation of the fall and redemption of the human race. The traveller who 'fell among thieves' is to be understood as Adam, who fell victim to the tricks and temptations of the devil. Just as the man in the parable was robbed, stripped and left half dead, so Adam was deprived of his innocence and his place in paradise, and was cast out with the threat of eternal death hanging over him. The priest and the Levite, who failed to help him in his plight, stand for the Jewish religion, which had failed to rescue fallen humanity. The Samaritan represents Jesus Christ, providing the salvation which the old religion had failed to secure. The medicinal oil and wine symbolize God's grace and Christ's blood, which he shed to take away the sin of the world. The inn where the traveller is taken to recuperate is the Church, the innkeeper is Saint Paul, representing the Church's ministers, and the two coins are the two sacraments of baptism and eucharist, by which the Church brings the fruits of salvation to its members. The Samaritan's promised return is the second coming of Christ, at which time all the Church's faithful ministers will receive the due reward for their labours.

Is that true? It is true that the parable was interpreted and preached along those lines for a thousand years. It is true that the summary given above is a fair outline of the Church's traditional teaching on the fall and redemption of our race. It is also true that the elements in the story match the relevant elements of Christian doctrine. So in a sense, yes, it is true. But I personally doubt whether it is true that Jesus told the story with that interpretation in mind, or that Luke wrote it down with the intention that it would be understood in that way. So – if I am right about this – there is another sense in which the parable, so interpreted, is not true.

Look again at the whole passage, Luke 10.25–37. It gives not only the parable itself but its setting. This is important, because the Good Samaritan is a story within a story, and it can be argued that the true meaning of the parable is going to be the one that makes best sense in that wider context. Jesus related the incident in answer to a question, 'And who is my neighbour?'

and he immediately followed it up with a further question, 'Which of these three, do you think, was a neighbour to the man who fell into the hands of the robbers?' (Luke 10.29, 36). When given the answer, 'The one who showed him mercy', he then issued the command, 'Go and do likewise' (Luke 10.37). From the perspective of the larger story, therefore, the truth of the parable is going to be related to its teaching on neighbour-liness. Approached in this way, the take-home message of the story is a moral one, and so any judgement about its truth will have to be a moral one also. That is the reason that I personally doubt whether an allegorical and doctrinal interpretation, of the kind outlined above, was in the mind of the parable's author. Some parables are free-standing pieces of teaching that show up in different contexts in different Gospels (or even the Epistles). The Good Samaritan appears only here, and it is too well interwoven with its setting for me to doubt that it was composed for just this situation. But who composed it?

I argued above (drawing an analogy with the novels of Dickens) that the message of the parable could still be true, even if the incidents described in it were not historical. I think that most readers would agree with this assessment. So here is another question. If that is true of the story 'within the story', is it equally true of the wider story in which it is set? Let's assume we can agree that the message of the parable is true, even if the incident it describes never happened, but was invented by Jesus to illus-trate a point. Can we apply the same reasoning to the 'wider story', and say that the message of the parable will still be true, even if the incident that describes Jesus telling it never took place, but was invented by Luke to illustrate a point?

My guess is that many readers who were quite comfortable with the first step will be decidedly uncomfortable with the second one. It is one thing to accept that Jesus made up stories about unknown travellers. It is quite another to claim that Luke made up stories about Jesus himself. Yet I believe this is the most likely explanation of the Gospel record that we have. As in previous chapters of this book, a comparison between the Gospels, and a willingness to take the implications of what their writers leave out as seriously as what they include, will supply the evidence.

In large part it is the popularity and familiarity of the Good Samaritan that makes us recoil from the suggestion that Jesus himself did not compose it. That is natural. But, ironically, those very characteristics also supply one of the strongest arguments for believing that he may not in fact have told the story himself. Look at Matthew 22.34–40 and Mark 12.28–34. They are not identical with Luke 10.25–28, but they are sufficiently similar for us to assume that they relate to the same original incident. Such variations as we find are quite typical of the styles of the three writers: Mark has the longest account (see p. 29) above; Matthew adds a characteristic reminder of the continuing importance of 'all the law and the prophets' (Matthew 22.40; cf. 5.17–20); Luke has Jesus make the lawyer answer his own question (Luke 10.26; cf. 10.36). So why is there no mention in Matthew or Mark of the lawyer's supplementary question, 'And who is my neighbour?' (Luke 10.29), or of the story of the Good Samaritan that Jesus told in response to it? As with the nativity stories, as with the full Lord's Prayer, as with the opening up of the roof for the paralysed man, as with the second feeding miracle, as with every other example we might find of one or more of the Gospels leaving something out, it is always possible to give the explanation: 'It did happen, but this or that evangelist either did not know about it or else chose to omit it for reasons best known to himself.' That is always possible. Arguments from silence can never be conclusive. But I hope we have seen enough so far in this book to show that some creative activity on the part of the evangelists is a possible and, indeed, a probable explanation of some inconsistencies and other difficulties facing a purely historical approach to the Gospels. I hope that by now it goes without saying that this does not imply any intention to deceive on the part of the evangelists. Quite the reverse. They and their readers believed their writing was being done under the inspiration of the risen Lord himself, and that their words were his words. Just as the Lord's Prayer may properly bear that title, even if we decide that its composition was achieved through Matthew, so the Good Samaritan is no less the Lord's parable because it was scripted by his servant and evangelist Luke.

With that in mind, I want now to pursue seriously the idea

that Luke is the only Gospel to tell the story of the Good Samaritan because it was Luke himself who composed it. What positive evidence is there to support this claim? First, it is a fully developed narrative, not just a short illustration, and second, it is a 'human interest' story. These are both common features of the parables found in Luke's Gospel only – see Luke 15.11–32 (Prodigal Son); 16.1–9 (Dishonest Steward); 16.19–31 (Rich Man and Lazarus). Whether Luke composed all these parables himself, or whether he alone among the evangelists selected from a received collection of stories told originally by Jesus, they are evidence of his bias in favour of stories of this type. Further, as we have seen, the Good Samaritan is most naturally understood as a straightforward example of how we should behave, rather than as an allegorical parable with a coded message. This is again typical of Luke-only parables, for instance the parables on prayer at Luke 18.1–14 (Unjust Judge; Pharisee and Tax-collector). Another Lucan trait is to show traditional 'underdogs' in a good light (e.g. the widow and the tax-collector in the examples just given), and here we find one of the despised Samaritans as the hero of the story (as is also the case in the healing of the ten lepers, Luke 17.11–19, a healing story not found in the other Gospels). Turning from the parable to its immediate setting, we have already noted how Jesus twice asks questions to draw the lawyer out. This technique is also used to good effect at Luke 7.36–50 (at Simon the Pharisee's house, another exchange not recorded by the other Gospels). None of this proves that Luke composed the Good Samaritan, but it does suggest that if he were to write a parable, it is just the sort of parable that he would write.

Having established that the style and much of the detail of the story are very typical of Luke, we still need to find some reason why he should have decided to write this story and put it in at this place. One cannot be certain, but a likely answer is to be found in the piece of dialogue that is reported in Mark's Gospel at just this point. In Mark's account, the scribe does not ask a supplementary question, as Luke's lawyer does. He affirms Jesus' answer by saying, 'You are right, Teacher,' and then going on to repeat what Jesus has himself just said, adding at the end: ' "to love one's neighbour as oneself," – this is much more important than all whole burnt offerings and sacrifices' (Mark 12.32–33). Luke's story can be seen as an illustration of that theme. The Samaritan who shows mercy to the needy man is fulfilling God's will much more than the temple officials – the priest and the Levite – who are too busy about their sacrificial duties to do an act of simple human kindness.

So, after all that, is the story of the Good Samaritan true? And what does it mean to say that it is true? For the reasons given, I believe on balance that neither the events within the story nor the immediate context of the story were historical events in the lives of the characters portrayed in them – neither the traveller and the Samaritan, nor the lawyer and Jesus – but that none the less the story is true because its moral message is true. And an integral part of the parable's message is: that the abstract moral teaching will become completely true for us only when we take it to heart and obey the command, 'Go and do likewise.'

We have now come a long way from our starting-point of treating the Gospels seriously as eyewitness accounts, so I want to reiterate: all that we have discovered and proposed has grown naturally and necessarily out of that beginning. At various points along the way a decision has had to be made on a balance of probabilities. In the case of the Good Samaritan, we have to weigh the likelihood that Luke composed the parable himself against two rival possibilities: either that Matthew and Mark deliberately omitted it from the teachings of Jesus known to them, or else that the parable was somehow lost from the tradition before it reached them, and came to Luke by some more or less secret route. For the reasons already given, I find the theory of Lucan authorship the more likely of these explanations. Those who are less persuaded than I am of the significance of the silences and omissions of the Gospels may choose to weigh the probabilities differently. There is nothing wrong with that. What I believe there is something wrong with is the refusal even to acknowledge those difficulties which stand in the way of treating the evangelists simply as chroniclers of events in Jesus' life. Equally, I believe it is improper to refuse to accept the witness of the Gospels simply on the grounds that 'miracles don't happen' or 'science has proved all that to be nonsense'. Between those two extremes I have attempted to steer a middle course, and to share with the reader some of the tools and skills required for that task. All those skills will now be needed as we turn to the most dramatic of all Jesus' signs and wonders: the raising of Lazarus.

11

Lazarus

Read: John 11.1–44

Apart from the resurrection of Jesus himself, the raising of Lazarus is the most spectacular of all the signs, wonders or miracles which are recorded in the New Testament. There are other stories of the dead (or apparently dead) being restored – Jairus' daughter (Matthew 9.18–26; Mark 5.21–43; Luke 8.40–56) and the widow of Nain's son (Luke 7.11–17) by Jesus; Dorcas (Acts 9.36–42) by Peter; Eutychus (Acts 20.7–12) by Paul – but none of these patients had already been buried, and it is questionable whether they were actually dead. In fact, in the best-known case – Jairus' daughter – Jesus clearly states that she was not dead, but only sleeping. Lazarus is altogether different: he has been dead and buried for four days, and – as his sister Martha succinctly puts it in the Authorized Version – 'By this time he stinketh!' (John 11.39).

Even when allowance is made for the first century being a more credulous age than our own, a time when miracles of all kinds were accepted as part of day-to-day life, it has to be acknowledged that the raising of Lazarus was something special. Even if we are prepared to accept all the miracles of Jesus at face value, this one still stands out as exceptional. So how is it that no other New Testament writer so much as mentions the existence of Lazarus (see note at the end of this chapter, p. 85), let alone refers to his being raised from the dead after four days in the tomb? That is the most serious difficulty with this story. On at least three counts, we should expect it to feature in any history of the life and work of Jesus. First, it is an exceedingly noteworthy episode in its own right. Spectacular is not too strong a word. Second, it is, according to John, the event which led directly to the excitement generated in Jerusalem on what we now call 'Palm Sunday'. All four Gospels record the events of that day (Matthew 21.1–9; Mark 11.1–10; Luke 19.28–38; John 12.12–19), so it is strange that only one of them should give an account of this marvellous sign of God's power working in Jesus, which was the cause of the crowd's having gathered in the first place (John 12.17–18). Third, again according to John, it was the raising of Lazarus that ignited and fuelled the determination of the Pharisees and chief priests to secure Jesus' own death (John 11.45–53). Any one of these facts would make the absence of the Lazarus story from the other three Gospels surprising. Together they make it astounding.

It is this silence, not any modern scepticism about the possibility of miracles, which stands powerfully in the way of accepting John's account as straightforward history. The appearance of a parable or a miracle or a piece of teaching in only one of the four Gospels may have any number of innocent explanations. We have already discussed the need to accept that historians and biographers will be selective, and sometimes three of the four evangelists may well have chosen to exclude a particular episode, or indeed have been ignorant of it. But that can hardly be the case here. If the event took place, in the manner John relates and with the consequences he describes, then the historical reliability of all the other Gospels is thrown into very serious doubt by their failure to record it. It would be the equivalent – only far more serious – of writing a life of Churchill and not saying he became the wartime prime minister, or of Jane Austen and omitting any mention of *Pride and Prejudice*. If, on the other hand, the event did not take place as reported, where does that leave John? I have previously suggested that Matthew may have compiled the Lord's Prayer and that Luke may have composed the parable of the Good Samaritan. We have even looked at the possibility that Mark may have been responsible for the daring tale of the four friends of the paralysed man, who are said to have ripped up the very roof of the house in which Jesus was sitting and teaching. But none of these pieces of alleged creative writing by the evangelists is on a scale to be compared with inventing the raising of Lazarus. Yet we are faced with an unavoidable dilemma: if the miracle did happen, how could the synoptics possibly have left it out? And if it did not happen, how did John have the audacity to put it in? Can the reputation for truthfulness of all four Gospels be salvaged from this apparent impasse? I believe it can, but only by adopting one of two approaches, neither of which is without difficulties.

The first way to tackle the problem would be to make the historical reliability of the Gospels' positive statements an unquestionable assumption, and to explain their (to us) inexplicable omissions as part of the divine economy. After all, writing materials were expensive in the first century, and in any case there were physical limits on the length of scrolls. (There is some quite good evidence that Christians were responsible for the development of the 'codex', as the modern book format is called, in order to have their holy books in a more accessible form. But the original Gospels would most probably have been in scroll form.) I have said in an earlier chapter (p. 26) that we should not discount such mundane and practical explanations as to why the Gospels are as they are. There is nothing inherently unhistorical or unscientific in assuming that God's overruling providence ensured that an important story such as the raising of Lazarus was recorded by one evangelist, and left out by the others to save space. Unfortunately this suggestion does run up against a lack of consistency: it explains why in cases such as this and the Good Samaritan there is no duplication, but creates a problem out of all the many other places where two or more Gospels do tell the same story, sometimes in virtually identical words. Where, in particular, would it leave the feeding of the multitude, which as we saw appears no less than six times in four Gospels?

The alternative approach to the problem is to assume that John alone records this story because the other three did not know about it. And the only plausible explanation for how that could be is that it did not take place. Stories can convey important truths without being historical accounts. We saw that Jesus' tale of the Good Samaritan, for example, may have recounted an actual incident on the Jericho road, but the truth of its message about loving our neighbour is quite independent of that. Most probably the story was just made up to put over that message. But, as we admitted when discussing this in the last chapter, it is one thing to invent a parable about an anonymous traveller, but an entirely different matter to start 'making up' stories about Jesus. All the same, we have found it necessary to take seriously the second possibility. For instance, we have already seen an apparent willingness on the part of Matthew and Luke to fill out the details of Jesus' birth, so maybe John is writing in a similarly creative way about the events leading to his death. There are some clues in the details of the story which point in this direction.

One possible way to consider the episode is to see it as an acted parable, illustrating in a dramatic story some of the truths about Jesus which the evangelist has already set out as more formal teaching. For example, at the very start of John's Gospel it was said of the Word of God that 'in him was life' (John 1.4) and that he 'became flesh and lived among us, and we have seen his glory' (John 1.14). In the raising of Lazarus, John shows Jesus, the Word-made-flesh, bringing life to one who was dead – and doing it 'for God's glory, so that the Son of God may be glorified' (John 11.4).

Again, John has already reported Jesus as saying that, 'the hour is coming and is now here when the dead will hear the voice of the Son of God, and those who hear will live' (John 5.25). This is vividly demonstrated by Lazarus: 'he [Jesus] cried with a loud voice, "Lazarus, come out!" The dead man came out' (John 11.43–44).

Another feature to notice is the way the raising of Lazarus compares and contrasts with John's account of the resurrection of Jesus himself. The evangelist seems determined to underline the contrast between the active Jesus and the passive Lazarus. Thus Jesus had to order the removal of the stone from the tomb of his friend (John 11.39) whereas, when Mary Magdalene came to his own tomb on the first Easter morning, she saw that the stone had already been removed (John 20.1). And while the grave-clothes of Jesus were left lying in the empty sepulchre (John 20.6–7), Lazarus came forth (being carried?) still wrapped up like a mummy, so that Jesus had to give the order, 'Unbind him, and let him go' (John 11.44). This all emphasizes Jesus' earlier teaching, as reported by John, in relation to his own life: 'I have power to lay it down, and I have power to take it up again' (John 10.18).

We have a natural uneasiness about the suggestion that John might deliberately create an 'historical' incident as noteworthy as this simply in order to illustrate a theological truth (even so profound a truth as the victory of God's love over the destructive power of death). I am not sure whether that uneasiness should be increased or alleviated by the discovery that he is probably not alone among the evangelists in thus 'creating' a resurrection scene. There is in Matthew's Gospel an often overlooked pair of verses immediately after the account of the crucifixion, which read as follows: 'The tombs also were opened, and many bodies of the saints who had fallen asleep were raised. After his resurrection they came out of the tombs and entered the holy city and appeared to many' (Matthew 27.52–53).

It is a passage not much discussed in debates about the resurrection, nor celebrated in Christian art. (The only example known to me which centres on this scene is a painting called 'The Risen Christ' by Anton Andreievitch Ivanoff, reproduced on an Easter card I recently received. Jesus is approaching a group of resurrected figures in varying states of dishabille, with John the Baptist featuring prominently in his traditional garb and familiar 'Behold, the Lamb of God' pose.) However, like the little-read conversation in the boat, which proved so crucial to our understanding of the feeding of the five thousand (see p. 57 above), this largely ignored incident reported by Matthew is surely of the utmost importance. It raises exactly the same kinds of questions as the Lazarus episode. True, it is less central to Matthew's account than Lazarus is to John's, but in its way it is even more remarkable. Not one corpse only but 'many bodies of the saints' were involved, and they 'appeared to many' in Jerusalem itself, not just in some outlying village. If this is an historically reliable happening, then how is it that only one evangelist mentions it, and he only as an aside? And what about the authorities? Bribing the soldiers about one empty tomb (see Matthew 28.11–15) might be possible, but how would they explain dozens or hundreds of them? So we are faced with the question: did the multiple resurrections recorded by Matthew happen as he says they did or not?

My hunch is that many people – both scholars and ordinary Christians – who give a generally high rating to the historical reliability of the Gospels, would in this case drift towards a vague notion of its being a later legendary accretion. For myself, I do not believe in such anonymous 'legends'. There is no evidence that Matthew 27.52–53 is a later addition to the Gospel, and I believe that either it happened as he says, or else Matthew himself created the story to illustrate a theological point. It is fundamentally the same point that Paul made to the Corinthians in words that are very well known: 'Christ has been raised from the dead, the first fruits of those who have died ... for as all die in Adam, so all will be made alive in Christ' (1 Corinthians 15.20–22). I could not disprove the legend theory, but I find it unsatisfactory as an explanation. It suggests that the story (a) is not true and (b) somehow got into the Gospel by accident. In other words, it is just the kind of negative response that drives many intelligent people to feel that only if the Gospels are historically accurate can they have anything of positive value to tell us. By contrast, if Matthew created the story, even though it could not be called historically accurate, it was most certainly composed to illustrate a theological truth. And it certainly did not get there by accident: it is a deliberate proclamation of Matthew's faith in Christ's victory over death. To my mind, that is altogether more satisfactory.

We now have two cases of resurrection stories – John's Lazarus at Bethany and Matthew's saints in Jerusalem – which offer the modern Christian a hard choice: either to accept that they were created by their authors, or else to find a plausible reason for the complete lack of any other reference to such amazing occurrences having taken place. For me the existence of two examples swings the probability in favour of the evangelists' creative writing. Negatively, it is harder to explain the absence of evidence for two stories than for one; positively, if two evangelists were engaged in this kind of dramatic presentation of theology, then it increases the likelihood that such an approach was considered acceptable both to the writers and to the first generation of readers of the Gospels.

Let me say yet again that this is not a view which arises from any predisposition to disbelieve the literal truth of the Gospels. It has come about as a result of considering the consequences of taking the historical truth of the New Testament accounts with the utmost seriousness. Where it does perhaps differ from some other investigations is in extending that seriousness to the unexplained silences. Like the non-barking dog in the Sherlock Holmes story, this silent witness may prove crucial to a full understanding of the purpose and method of the evangelists, and of their perception of the truth.

Lazarus, Martha and Mary in Luke's Gospel

Some commentators point to similarities between the hero of the story of 'Lazarus and the Rich Man' in Luke 16.19–31 and Lazarus of Bethany. First, they share the same name, which is the Greek/Latin form of the popular Jewish name Eleazer, meaning 'God has helped'. Second, though we know little about either of them, we do know that both of them died in the course of the Gospel narrative. Third, one was raised from the dead and the other – although not actually raised – does have the possibility of his returning from the dead discussed within the story. Against these similarities, the circumstances of the two men and the details of their stories are quite different. Apart from anything else, the Lucan story is nowadays universally regarded as a parable, a fictional story composed by a teacher to make a point, whereas Lazarus and his sisters are generally taken to be historical characters.

Mention of Lazarus' sisters brings us to a related coincidence (if such it is) between Luke and John. Elsewhere Luke does mention two sisters, Mary and Martha, but this confuses rather than clarifies the situation. These sisters live not in Bethany but in an unnamed village in another part of the country (Luke 10.38), and there is no mention of their having a brother. The characters of the two sisters (active fussy Martha contrasted with quieter contemplative Mary) do tally in the two Gospels, but that is not enough to prove they are the same people. And even if they were, that does nothing to support the identification of the Lazarus in Luke's parable (whose brothers are mentioned, but no sisters) with the Lazarus of Bethany.

12

The anointing of Jesus

Read: Matthew 26.6–13; Mark 14.3–9; Luke 7.36–50; John 12.1–8

To those who have been working through this book in order, the anointing of Jesus might almost seem too good to be true. Had I been able to create for myself a Gospel incident, specially designed to illustrate all the problems raised in the preceding chapters, I could hardly have done better than to produce this one. Stories such as Jesus' baptism and the feedings of the multitude have accustomed us to the idea that certain Gospel passages display both significant similarities and significant differences, and that either one or two original events might lie behind these accounts. The story of the anointing now raises the spectre of no less than three similar yet different incidents in the course of Jesus' ministry.

In all four passages Jesus is the guest at a meal, in the course of which a woman anoints him with ointment – an action which gives rise to criticism. No other details are common to all four Gospels: Matthew 26.6–13 and Mark 14.3–9 are closely similar and may be treated as a single version; Luke 7.36–50 and John 12.1–8 differ in important respects both from Matthew/Mark and from each other. There are also matters of detail in which, at different points, each of the three accounts finds itself the 'odd one out' compared with the other two. It will be useful to consider some of these details.

Matthew/Mark and John both place the incident in the village of Bethany shortly before the Passover festival at which Jesus will be crucified. In each case the evangelist precedes the account of the anointing with an announcement that the Jewish authorities are engaged in plans to arrest and kill Jesus. Luke's story is placed much earlier, during the Galilean phase of Jesus' ministry. Although neither the time nor the place is given exactly, the former is certainly not the week leading up to the crucifixion and the latter is most unlikely to be Bethany, which is not in the northern region of Galilee but in the southern province of Judea, close to Jerusalem.

There is just a possibility of reading into Luke's account a detour at Bethany. At Luke 7.17, following the raising of the widow's son at Nain, there is a reference to Jesus' fame spreading 'throughout Judea'. This could be taken to imply that Jesus temporarily moved south at this time, out of Galilee and into Judea, but that is an unlikely interpretation. First, there is no specific reference to Jesus being in Judea at this point in the story. Second, the references to Capernaum and Nain (in chapter 7) and to Jesus' family and the crossing of the lake (in chapter 8) suggest an unbroken presence in the north. Third, at Luke 4.44, Luke says that Jesus toured 'the synagogues of Judea'. Judea is used here by Luke whereas the parallel passages in Matthew and Mark have Jesus in 'Galilee' (Matthew 4.23; Mark 1.39). This suggests that Luke uses the term 'Judea' in a rather loose way to refer to 'the land of the Jews' generally, including Galilee, rather than just to the southern province to which the name strictly applies. At all events, a very strained reading of Luke's narrative is required in order to place his anointing episode outside Galilee.

Turning our attention to the Gospels that place the story in Bethany, we still find a disagreement as to its precise location. According to John, the meal was served by Martha, the sister of Lazarus, and there is no suggestion that it was held anywhere other than at their home (John 12.1–2). Matthew/Mark locates the meal 'in the house of Simon the leper' (Matthew 26.6; Mark 14.3). It is interesting that Luke, who initially refers to Jesus' host simply as 'one of the Pharisees', later names him as Simon (Luke 7.36, 39–40). Since Simon the 'leper' had presumably recovered from his leprosy (otherwise he would hardly have been in a position to give dinner parties) it is possible that he is the same person as Simon the Pharisee. This would reduce the muddle a little, but even allowing for this, we are still faced with a multiplicity of choices: was the meal held in the house of Simon or of Lazarus? If it was Simon's, was this house in Bethany or somewhere in Galilee? And did the occasion take place early in Jesus' ministry or within a day or two of his death?

The next question to arise is the identification of the central character. A pious tradition in the Western Church – a tradition dating back at least to Pope Gregory the Great in the sixth century – has added a further layer of confusion to the whole business by identifying the woman who anointed Jesus with Mary Magdalene. (The Eastern Orthodox Church has never accepted the identification and, with the revised calendar of 1969, it has now been officially dropped by the Roman Catholic Church as well. It is, however, still a strong tradition among the faithful.) Mary Magdalene is mentioned by name at various places in all four Gospels (e.g. Matthew 27.56; Mark 15.40; Luke 8.2; John 20.1), but none of them names her here. Matthew/Mark simply refers to 'a woman' (Matthew 26.7; Mark 14.3); Luke calls her 'a woman in the city, who was a sinner' (Luke 7.37); John names her as 'Mary' (John 12.3) and presumably intends us to infer that she is the same Mary whose sister Martha was (by his account) serving the meal and whose brother was Lazarus. Matters are further complicated by the sisters Mary and Martha who appear in Luke 10.38–42. They may or may not be the same pair as Lazarus' sisters (but most likely are not – see the discussion above, p. 85). Certainly Luke makes no cross-reference between this Mary and his 'woman in the city, who was a sinner', and neither of them is identified with Mary Magdalene.

Whoever she was, all four Gospels agree that the woman brought ointment to Jesus. Other details vary (see Matthew 26.7; Mark 14.3; Luke 7.37–38; John 12.3). Matthew, Mark and Luke all say it was in an alabaster jar; Matthew, Mark and John note it was very precious; Mark and John identify it as 'nard'; Matthew and Mark report that it was poured over Jesus' head (Mark alone telling us the jar was broken in the process), while Luke and John agree that she used it to anoint his feet, which she also wiped with her hair; Luke alone describes how she first washed his feet with her tears and then kissed them. John comments on the way the fragrance filled the house.

Some of these variations, such as the reference to value, are trivial when it comes to the task of reconstructing the scene. Others, such as whether the head or feet were anointed, are more significant. Luke's reference to weeping and kissing is important for the way the story develops in his particular case. What is of interest is the way in which – unlike most of the other examples we have looked at – the agreements and disagreements seem to range randomly across all four accounts. If there was more than one incident behind the four accounts, then one cannot simply say that Gospel W is based on incident Y and Gospel X on incident Z. They are all jumbled up. If, on the other hand, they are all based on a single event, we may reasonably ask how and why the differences came about.

In each of our four accounts the anointing gives rise to criticism. In Matthew, Mark and John the substance of the discussion is the same: the woman is blamed for not selling the precious ointment and giving the proceeds to the poor; Jesus defends her by referring to his burial and pointing out that, 'You always have the poor with you, but you do not always have me' (Matthew 26.11; Mark 14.7; John 12.8).

Luke is at this point quite different. Gone is the accusation of wastefulness against the woman. Gone is the reference to selling the ointment and giving to the poor (explaining, perhaps, why Luke alone failed earlier to comment on the extreme value of the perfume). Gone also is Jesus' own reference to his forthcoming burial. This ties in with the setting of Luke's account early in Jesus' ministry rather than on the eve of his passion. In place of these missing elements, there is in Luke a charge laid against Jesus himself, one which could only apply in this version of the story because only Luke has portrayed the woman as 'a sinner' (Luke 7.37). In response, Jesus gives his host a lesson on forgiveness and love and pronounces the woman absolved from her sins (Luke 7.40–50).

My approach in this book has been to encourage an acceptance of the inherent problems that are found when treating the Gospels as historical records. I have tried to point beyond the elusive 'facts of the case' to the different levels of truth enshrined in the Gospel stories themselves. So our aim has not been to find out the 'historical truth' behind the divergent accounts we have studied, but rather to learn to live without that kind of information. I firmly believe this is the right way to use the Bible, but I can also appreciate the curiosity that asks, 'Yes, but given all that, how did these different and sometimes conflicting versions of Jesus' words and actions come about?' So what follows is one possible explanation for the variations in the anointing story.

Because we have to start somewhere, I am making the assumption that there was a single historical incident underlying this story and that it happened essentially as Matthew and Mark record it. This is not the only possible starting-place but it is the simplest. It is also perfectly reasonable: their joint account is internally consistent and perfectly plausible. If it were not for the other two divergent versions, we should have no reason to question its reliability. So the task is to explain how the apparently contradictory stories told by Luke and John might have come about as developments of the original in Matthew/Mark.

We begin with John, because he is closer than Luke to what I take to be the historical case. He knew that the incident took place at Bethany and that the whole anointing story, as told in Matthew/Mark, was a foreshadowing of Jesus' death and burial. John had just used a long section of his Gospel telling the story of Lazarus of Bethany, which was itself presented by him as a parallel to Jesus' own death and burial and resurrection (see pp. 82 above). It is easy enough to understand why he might have changed the venue of the anointing from the house of the unknown Simon to that of Lazarus, and identified the unknown woman as one of his sisters. For John, the truth of the anointing story lay in its relationship to Jesus' passion and resurrection; by increasing the strength of that relationship he deepened its truth.

The change from anointing the head to anointing the feet is made by both John and Luke, so the question arises: did they make the change independently or did one take the idea from the other? Either is possible. My own view is that John was familiar with Luke's Gospel (this is a contentious opinion that I do not have space here to defend) and took the variation from there. In Luke the woman used her hair to dry Jesus' feet before anointing them. John has Mary wipe off the ointment with her hair. This is a rather strange detail and makes more sense if we imagine John working at this point from Luke's version of events. He deletes the reference to washing Jesus' feet with tears (John has a better feet-washing story lined up for the next chapter, see John 13.1–11) but fails to notice the effect this has on the hair reference. Against this view are two possible objections. One is the general opinion among scholars that John was unfamiliar with Luke's Gospel. The other is a curious 'forward reference' to this incident at the beginning of the Lazarus story, where the sick man's sister Mary is identified as 'the one who anointed the Lord with perfume and wiped his feet with her hair' (John 11.2). I call this reference curious because the anointing has not yet happened, and so this description of Mary will mean nothing to someone reading John's Gospel for the first time. This inconsistency – especially when combined with the repeated emphasis on the perfume, feet and hair – might betray some deeper significance to the scene in John's mind, which is quite independent of Luke's account. I don't know. Another signpost to dig for hidden treasure, perhaps?

Making Judas the one who complains about the woman is unique to John (John 12.4), but is consistent with Matthew saying it was 'the disciples' (Matthew 26.8) and with Mark, who simply refers to 'some who were there' (Mark 14.4). It could be historically accurate or it could just be John picking on a likely suspect. He does treat Judas more harshly than the other evangelists, accusing him of being not only a traitor but also a thief (John 12.4, 6).

Luke's story, as we have seen, is significantly different in that it centres on the character of the woman as a penitent sinner. This combines themes dear to Luke's heart. First, there is his fondness for bringing women into his narrative. Among his references to women where they get no corresponding mention in the other Gospels are the following: the concentration on Mary and the inclusion of Elizabeth and Anna in the account of Jesus' birth (Luke 1—2); the widow of Nain (Luke 7.11–17); Joanna and Susanna (Luke 8.2–3); Mary and Martha (Luke 10.38–42); the woman in the crowd (Luke 11.27–28); the healing of the bent woman (Luke 13.10–17); the woman who lost a coin (Luke 15.1–10); the importunate widow (Luke 18.1–8); the women of Jerusalem (Luke 23.27–31). Second, the penitent sinner is also a favourite subject. For example, the following appear only in Luke: the prodigal son (Luke 15.11–32); the tax-collector at prayer (Luke 18.9–14); Zacchaeus (Luke 19.1–10); the 'penitent' thief (Luke 23.39–43).

The contrast of the sinner who is praised by Jesus with the Pharisee who is rebuked echoes the parable of the Pharisee and the tax-collector at prayer (Luke 18.9–14). The woman's position behind Jesus (Luke 7.38) and the fact that she anoints his feet rather than his head (as in the Matthew/Mark account) indicate a humility and caution that remind us of the woman who touched the hem of Jesus' garment from behind in the anonymity of the crowd (Matthew 9.20; Mark 5.27; Luke 8.44), in order to receive healing. The theme of forgiveness also calls to mind the paralysed man (Matthew 9.2–8; Mark 2.3–12; Luke 5.18–26). That Luke might have had both these stories in mind is indicated by the dialogue at the end of the story: 'Then he [Jesus] said to her, "Your sins are forgiven." But those who were at the table with him began to say among themselves, "Who is this who even forgives sins?" And he said to the woman, "Your faith has saved you, go in peace"' (Luke 7.48–50). The onlookers' questioning of the fact that Jesus forgives sins matches the similar remarks in the story of the paralytic; and the slightly inappropriate closing words of Jesus to the woman (inappropriate since they refer to faith, and all the emphasis up to this point has been on love) come from the story of the woman who touched the hem of his garment.

None of this proves that the Lucan account is not of an historical occasion – as I said, there is no way to prove what the historical reality behind this set of stories really was. What I have done, as with the Good Samaritan, is to indicate reasons for thinking that if Luke were to write a story based on the Bethany anointing story in Matthew/Mark, then this is the sort of story we should expect him to write. More generally, I have tried to indicate one possible way in which the accounts we have could have arisen, given what we have learned of the methods and interests of the four evangelists.

13

Gospel truth

At the start of this book I suggested we begin by taking the Gospels seriously as 'eyewitness accounts of events in the life of Jesus'. I intended this to be an uncontroversial opening. Yet the very first person to read my manuscript – a theologian who has written on the subject of Jesus and the Gospels – reacted strongly against such a proposal. According to this scholar, such a description of the Gospels 'needs so much qualification as to be robbed of all regular meaning'. This response is a vivid illustration of the great gulf between those who study the Gospels professionally and those who hear them read Sunday by Sunday in church or stumble across them, courtesy of the Gideons, in a hotel bedroom. What I have tried to do in these chapters is to begin to bridge that gulf.

New Testament scholars are, for the most part, practising Christians whose aim is to understand and proclaim the gospel, not to destroy it. They live daily with the difficulties facing a straightforward historical approach to the life of Jesus, and their work is dedicated to overcoming those problems. This involves modifying and even setting aside altogether the 'eye-witness account' approach. Alternative ways of interpreting the reported words and works of Jesus are developed. The gulf arises because most people outside this academic circle are not aware of those difficulties. So the hard-won solutions presented by the scholars are answering questions that nobody else is asking. At best, the scholars are seen as struggling with problems of their own making; at worst they are treated as enemies of Christ, seeking to avoid the challenge of faith themselves and to lead others astray.

The clergy, made aware of the problems by their own studies but rightly concerned not to put unnecessary stumbling-blocks in the way of the faithful, tend to play down the difficulties. For perfectly understandable reasons, they concentrate on the inward and spiritual meaning of the Gospel stories, rather than the outward – and often awkward – visible signs. Side-stepping the historical questions in this way works remarkably well for most of the time, but it can give out an unintended message to congregations that awkward questions should not be asked. It can also leave people vulnerable when those who really are hostile to Christianity decide to make capital out of the more obvious discrepancies and inconsistencies in the New Testament records.

So the limited aim of these studies in the Gospels has been to show that there is indeed a series of problems inherent in the historical approach. They are problems which are not of the scholars' own making, but ones to which they seek to provide answers. It has been a ground-clearing exercise. I have not tackled the difficulties head on or tried to solve them, but simply shown that they do exist and that they need not be detrimental to faith. I hope that the result will be readers who are more understanding of what the scholars are about, and more willing and able to benefit from what they have to say. All I shall attempt here is to indicate some of the alternative lines of approach which have been taken in the past or are currently being explored.

The early Christians had ready to hand two demonstrations of how to handle ancient and revered texts which contained obscure or trivial or embarrassing material. One was the way in which cultured pagans interpreted the early Greek writers, especially Homer, and the other was the way in which contemporary Jews interpreted the Old Testament. In both cases it was allegory which provided an important tool. Allegory involves taking details in one situation and applying them in a quite different one. The interpretation of the parable of the Sower (Mark 4.14–20) is a familiar example of the method. We see its application to Old Testament interpretation in the Letters of Paul, himself a Jewish scholar before becoming a Christian. The Law given to Moses included the command, 'You shall not muzzle an ox while it is treading out the grain' (Deuteronomy 25.4). We shall probably read this as an early example of animal rights: Let the poor beast eat a little of the corn while it is working. Paul sees things differently. Writing to the Corinthians he is scornful of the idea that God's real concern is for the oxen. The words were spoken, he writes, 'entirely for our sake' (1 Corinthians 9.10). Paul then interprets them as giving biblical (that is, divine) backing to his own claim that an apostle is entitled to be maintained by the Christian community while he is about the Lord's work. The same text is quoted to similar effect in 1 Timothy 5.17–18.

There are two immediate objections to using this kind of allegory to determine the truth of a Gospel passage. The first and more general one is that it opens the door to making the words of Scripture mean anything the commentator wishes. The other is that for early Christians the Gospels were not ancient writings like those attributed to Homer or Moses. They referred to events within living memory and needed no such devices to explain their meaning.

As to the second of these points, it appears that – for good or ill – once the Gospels became accepted as 'holy Scripture', then the same criteria were applied to their interpretation as to the much older writings of the Old Testament. Certainly by the fourth century AD, and probably much sooner, there was no appreciable difference between the Christian approaches to the books of the Old and of the New Testaments. In both cases, even the smallest details would be given a spiritual significance, which was taken to be their 'true' meaning. For instance, the five barley loaves used by Jesus to feed the five thousand (John 6.9) were taken to represent the five books of the Law of Moses. Barley loaves had hard, coarse crusts which made them difficult to break open and eat; in the same way – so the explanation went – the Jewish Law was hard to follow and understand until reinterpreted by Christ, when it yielded spiritual nourishment for the faithful. For the Christian preachers of the fourth century, that was the truth contained in the reference to those loaves. We saw the Good Samaritan receiving similar treatment on p. 73 above.

It is hard to resist the conclusion that such interpretations are more often read into the words of Scripture than drawn out of them. We may find them fascinating or irritating, depending on our taste, but we are unlikely today to treat them seriously as the deep 'truth' of the passage concerned, of more significance than the surface meaning of the words. Allegory used in this way, which is essentially arbitrary in its application of meanings, has long been abandoned as a serious means of biblical interpretation. In its day, however, it provided a crucial way to cope with errors and discrepancies that might otherwise have caused large parts of the Bible to be abandoned, and it should not be despised. Nor should it be confused with another method of interpretation with which it has some similarities and which we shall consider next: typology.

Typology is like allegory in that it draws parallels between two sets of events, but it generally involves a complex patterning and is less open to arbitrary interpretation. The significance of a New Testament character or event is explored by relating them to something in the Old Testament which already has a defined place within the biblical scheme of things. The overall effect is to add depth of meaning to both accounts and develop a rich interwoven tapestry of the entire Bible. My own studies have led me to believe that the Gospel writers themselves thought in this kind of way, which is why I have drawn attention to it – using the non-technical words 'patterning', 'foreshadowing' and 'fulfilling' – in the course of this book.

The central typology of the Christian Bible is that which sees in Jesus' death and resurrection the fulfilment of the Exodus of Israel out of Egypt. Again we can trace this back as far as Paul: 'Christ our passover is sacrificed for us: therefore let us keep the feast' (1 Corinthians 5.7; appointed in the Book of Common Prayer as the first words to be sung on Easter Day). Jesus thus becomes the 'true' Passover lamb, whose blood was shed that God's people might be delivered; the waters of the Red Sea, parting to allow the Israelites safely through, characterize 'the deep waters of death' through which Christ triumphantly passed. Nor does the pattern end there: the theme is carried through and applied also to the waters of baptism, through which succeeding generations of Christians pass as they become members of the Church and so claim their inheritance as true children of Israel and of God.

This approach to the Gospels says that the 'truth' of a given passage is not exhausted either by its superficial wording or by some hidden meaning requiring allegorical interpretation. Rather, the truth of the Gospels stretches back into the past and forward into the future, ever revealing new depths. The writers of the Old Testament had already linked the Exodus – the creation of the people of Israel – with the creation of the world out of the watery chaos which was 'in the beginning' (Genesis 1.1–2). Christians picked up on this theme and envisaged their crucified and risen Jesus there, 'in the beginning' (John 1.1–2, 14–18). In the other direction, as they looked forward to the end of all things, the same themes – life-giving water and Jesus the Lamb (Revelation 22.1–2) – set the pattern for the narrative.

In the modern era both allegory and typology gave way to a 'critical' approach to the Gospels, that is to say, an approach which treated them in the same way as any other ancient written text. Rather than assuming in advance that these were special writings with a special divinely inspired meaning, the critical approach was to treat them as ordinary books whose special character (if they indeed had one) would shine through of its own accord.

One important example of the modern method is 'source criticism'. This works on the assumption that identical pieces of writing cannot have come about by chance: either one must have been copied from the other, or else both were copied from some third document. A 'source', in this method of study, is defined as a written document copied by another writer. In the study of the Gospels, the most influential theory of source criticism has been the 'two document hypothesis'. This seeks to explain the connections between the three synoptic Gospels as follows. In passages where there is almost identical wording between Matthew, Mark and Luke, one may assume that Matthew and Luke were copying direct from Mark. Where there is almost identical wording between Matthew and Luke, but Mark either lacks the passage or is significantly different, one must assume that Matthew and Luke were both copying from some other book, now lost. The 'two documents' which give the hypothesis its name are thus the two written sources used by Matthew and Luke: one is Mark's Gospel (or, possibly, an earlier version of Mark's Gospel) and the other one, that has subsequently been lost, is usually given the name 'Q'. This is only one of several possible theories of sources for our Gospels, and is simply given here as an example. There are many variations on it.

Although still used by some scholars, the method of source criticism was at its height in the late nineteenth and early twentieth centuries. As time went on, its reliance on a theory of written sources was felt to be a weakness. Surely, people began to say, before ever the stories of Jesus were written down, they would have circulated by word of mouth. Scholars began to explore the implications of this fact. If there was an initial period of spoken or oral tradition, then the material we now have in our Gospels would already have begun to take shape before even the earliest written accounts were produced. So a new area of study opened up, known as 'form criticism', in which the Gospels were studied in order to identify a number of common 'forms' or types of short story. These were believed to have evolved in the earlier oral period of the Church's life and then provided the basic building-blocks for the later Gospel writers. Having identified the basic 'forms' of story, the form critics then tried to deduce the likely social and religious settings in which they developed. This exercise was bound up with the attempt to distinguish between sayings and contexts that went back to the earthly life of Jesus and those which were creations of the tradition (see note on the quest for the historical Jesus, p. 3 above). Form criticism flourished in the middle years of the twentieth century.

By degrees, source and form criticism led to the isolation of large parts of the Gospels that could be allocated to the evangelists' written and oral sources. The Gospels as we have them came to be regarded as mosaics of preconstructed pieces of teaching and biographical material relating to Jesus. Scholars then began to take an interest, really for the first time, in the contribution made by each of the individual Gospel writers. They examined both the 'cement', the connecting passages provided by the evangelists themselves to hold the received pieces of tradition together, and also the overall design of each Gospel. They noticed that the virtually identical story could be given two quite distinct 'spins' by placing it in two different contexts or altering just one or two words. This approach to Gospel study, because of its focus on the work of the evangelist as an editor or redactor, is called 'redaction criticism'. It was especially influential in the middle of the second half of the twentieth century.

With redaction criticism there came a move away from concentrating upon the sources of the words in the Gospels towards an interest in the literary structure of the books as a whole. This coincided with, and was in turn influenced by, a growing interest among biblical scholars in present-day literary criticism, and has resulted over the last twenty-five years in a spate of new disciplines such as 'narrative criticism', 'rhetorical criticism' and 'reader-response criticism'. With these developments one can detect the shift from a 'modern' to a 'postmodern' approach. The search for a single objective fact of the matter, whether in Jesus' precise words or the evangelist's editorial bias, gives way to a concern for the dynamic and living relationship between the writer, the characters in the story and the reader.

There is a sense in which the wheel has almost come full circle. Today's 'narrative theologians' do not seem a long way away from the typological approach, which I said above seems to be one largely adopted by the New Testament writers themselves. Narrative critics claim that the Gospel story of the life, death and resurrection of Jesus Christ, taken as a whole, provides the necessary and sufficient focus for the entire scriptural story of God, and they use typology as the technique for bringing other narratives into this focus. Old Testament tales are read as prefiguring the story of Jesus, and the Church's own story is told according to the Christ-pattern.

This approach, which depends upon the plausibility of finding a single 'story of God' running through the Bible, faces two kinds of criticism. First there are those who say that to find any one such story is in principle impossible, and that it can only be done by ignoring or distorting large parts of the Bible. Second, there are others who hold that the choice of any particular 'focal' story is bound to be arbitrary, so that narrative use of typology is no less subjective than using allegory. Such opponents of the method argue that using the Church's beliefs about Jesus (as set out in the creeds) as the basis for interpreting the 'Bible story' is to put the cart before the horse. Scripture, they say, should motivate doctrine, not the other way about. I think this complaint misses the point. If it were simply a case of subjecting biblical interpretation to doctrinal control, and then using the biblical 'evidence' to 'prove' the doctrine, that would certainly be a viciously circular argument. But not all circles are vicious. It is a good scientific approach to make an observation, create a hypothesis, make a prediction based upon it, and then test it. If the prediction is fulfilled, the hypothesis is confirmed, at least provisionally. That is a circular process, but a positive and benign one. And Christianity is rather like that.

When I say – as I do – that I believe the Gospels to be true, I do not mean that every item in the narrative is historically accurate. We have seen in these Bible studies that such a claim would, in a few cases, be impossible to maintain, and in many more it would be highly improbable. When I say that the Gospels are true I mean that their story is trustworthy, that the Christ-like pattern works: love conquers fear, good overcomes evil, life is not being rendered meaningless by death. All of this works out in practice, if we will let it. As a familiar hymn puts it:

> O make but trial of his love,
> Experience will decide
> How blest are they, and only they,
> Who in his truth confide.

('Through all the changing scenes of life', *New English Hymnal* no. 467)

Narrative criticism, in the hands of the scholars, can be a formidably technical matter, but I suspect that in the end it boils down to two very simple ideas: first, that people's lives can be transformed by a good story; and second, that this only comes about if – at some level – the story is reckoned by that person to be 'true'. My chief desire in writing this book is to increase the number of people who can, with full intellectual honesty, accept the Christian story – centred on the Gospels – as true. For some that will mean ignoring all the problems discussed in this book and taking the Gospels as wholly historically accurate. For others it will mean applying the tools of modern Gospel criticism to sift the historical from the 'legendary' or 'mythical' or whatever you like to call it. For others again, and this is where I would place myself, it means telling 'the old old story of Jesus and his love' and simply letting it work through its power as a story. The difference today from the past, I believe, is that we can now appreciate that there is not a single objective story of Jesus but many dynamic ones, because each one exists in relation to the person and the community by which it is told. Matthew, Mark, Luke and John have given us four such. It is for each of us to make our own.

Many years ago I heard a child psychologist say that when children ask of a story, 'Is it true?' they do not mean 'Is it historical?' but 'Could it happen to me?' Whether or not that is good developmental psychology I do not know, but it seems to me an excellent way of describing how Christian faith 'works' and what we mean by Gospel truth. The test is not whether the stories are historically accurate, but whether they can 'happen to me'. In other words, if I respond positively to the figure of Jesus in the Gospels, will I be able to see in my own life that transforming Christ-like pattern? I can only answer from my own experience – not least my experience over the past five years – that I am able to see it. And that for me is the treasure and the truth of the Gospels.

The Society for Promoting Christian Knowledge (SPCK) was founded in 1698. It has as its purpose three main tasks:

- **Communicating the Christian faith in its rich diversity**
- **Helping people to understand the Christian faith and to develop their personal faith**
- **Equipping Christians for mission and ministry**

SPCK Worldwide serves the Church through Christian literature and communication projects in over 100 countries. Special schemes also provide books for those training for ministry in many parts of the developing world. SPCK Worldwide's ministry involves Churches of many traditions. This worldwide service depends upon the generosity of others and all gifts are spent wholly on ministry programmes, without deductions.

SPCK Bookshops support the life of the Christian community by making available a full range of Christian literature and other resources, and by providing support to bookstalls and book agents throughout the UK. SPCK Bookshops' mail order department meets the needs of overseas customers and those unable to have access to local bookshops.

SPCK Publishing produces Christian books and resources, covering a wide range of inspirational, pastoral, practical and academic subjects. Authors are drawn from many different Christian traditions, and publications aim to meet the needs of a wide variety of readers in the UK and throughout the world.

The Society does not necessarily endorse the individual views contained in its publications, but hopes they stimulate readers to think about and further develop their Christian faith.

For further information about the Society, please write to:
SPCK, Holy Trinity Church, Marylebone Road,
London NW1 4DU, United Kingdom.
Telephone: 0171 387 5282